PANTYHOSE PARENTING

75 Common Sense Principles For Raising Kids

Geri Mauldin
with Don Huntington

PARK PLACE PUBLICATIONS
PACIFIC GROVE, CALIFORNIA

PANTYHOSE PARENTING
75 Common Sense Principles for Raising Kids

Geri Mauldin
with Don Huntington

© 2009 Elizabeth (Geri) Mauldin

ISBN 978-1-935530-00-8

First Edition
January 2010

Book designed by Patricia Hamilton
Original artwork by Santoshi Lama

Published by
Park Place Publications
P.O. Box 829
Pacific Grove, CA 93950
www.parkplacepublications.com

Printed in United States of America

Contents

Acknowledgements

I GIVE THE MAIN CREDIT for this book to the One "from whom all blessings flow." I thank Him for giving me the best husband I could possibly have found and four of the world's greatest children. I give Him credit for the wisdom He's given me and for the insights I've come to about living life and raising children.

I'm so thankful for my husband, Alan, who has been a rock for me to lean on. He is a man among men! I admire him for his integrity, passion, and devotion to the God whom we both serve.

I'm thankful to each of my children for being the source of so many of the lessons and insights that I've come to. They were my greatest teachers! They are my best friends!

I'm especially thankful to Don Huntington for listening to me and then writing exactly the book I would have written if I were a professional writer. (He told me he would do that and I have no idea how he actually pulled it off.)

Foreword

IF I HAD A DOLLAR BILL FOR every time someone told me that I should write a book and share with others my life experiences and the lessons that I've been able to learn from those experiences, I think I would have enough money for my husband and me to buy a nice meal in a restaurant with a menu written in French.

I'm a woman of faith and am perfectly confident that I have been led through life one step at a time and have been brought by hand to whatever wisdom and insights I have gained. I've been permitted to live in this world as though I were a child being homeschooled at the feet of an infinitely wise and loving Parent. I've applied myself to my lessons. I've learned wonderful things about this world.

Through this book I'm sharing with you the lessons about life and about raising children that I've learned from the experiences that He has led me to. Remember the words of the cowboy Sage, Will Rogers:

There are two kinds of people.
The one that learns by reading.
The few who learn by observation.

If you are the one "that learns by reading," then I'll guarantee that this book will save you from making some errors that you would otherwise make and from experiencing pains that would otherwise come to you.

Introduction

A FOUNDATIONAL PRINCIPLE OF GOOD parenting—and one that usually is not put into words—is that you have to pay the price to get the results from raising children.

Sometimes I think raising kids is like wearing pantyhose—which I believe to be a product probably created by some misogynist with a grudge against women. Women here in Northern California aren't wearing these things much any more, but a decade ago nothing was more common in a hen session than to hear women griping and complaining about putting on pantyhose. Nevertheless, we used to spend a lot of money each year buying these things, and then lying on our backs grunting and straining to put them on.

We did this because we wanted to make a nice-looking outfit look better. We put up with the aggravation because pantyhose helped us feel better about our appearance. So even though pantyhose made us uncomfortable, we put up with the pain for the sake of the payoff.

There's nothing comfortable about raising kids. There are a lot of wonderful things we could be doing with the time that we instead spend washing clothes, preparing meals, changing diapers, wiping snotty noses, disciplining, mediating conflicts, helping with homework—none of that is fun; most of it is not personally fulfilling. But we put up with the pain because of the payoff.

No matter how uncomfortable all that stuff makes us feel, we do it because if we raise them right, our children will make us look better. They will make us feel better about ourselves. Much more than any payoff we get from pantyhose, our children will help us face death with the knowledge that we've made changes in the world that will live on after we're gone.

When our kids were growing up, some parents thought we were too hard on them because we wouldn't let them join in some activities that we thought wouldn't promote the positive development of their character. Other parents thought we were too soft because, in their opinion, we would never rebuke our children with a stern voice or paddle them enough.

I think the "proof is in the pudding." Our kids have grown up to become fulfilled human beings with professions that bring them real satisfaction, plus they are raising happy families of their own and continue to have a deep love for each other and for us, their parents. At times the processes of child rearing were difficult, exhausting, and even overwhelming. But if I had it to do over again, I would cheerfully make those sacrifices all over again because I was laying the groundwork for the relationship that I now have with my children.

The process of raising my children to healthy adulthood did not come about by accident, but was the result of deliberate and conscious decisions and commitments made every day over the course of my entire life, beginning when I was a young person. I'm no pediatric behavioral specialist and have no degree in child studies. But I'm widely read and, most importantly, I'm a student of the human condition, blessed with a perceptive and analytical mind.

I've always had my eyes open to the world around me. From the time I was preparing for marriage until now, I've regarded life as being like a science project—one in which I could research to gain information about any particular challenge life was presenting me with, formulate an hypothesis about it, put the hypothesis to the test in deliberate action, and then either modify the hypothesis on the basis of the results or accept it as proven wisdom.

Through this deliberately reflective process I've learned how life works—how to do business, for example, and how to be a friend who is a friend indeed. I've especially learned how to create and maintain a home life such that my children could grow to be strong, independent human beings, learning to take their unique place in the world, finding their purpose in serving God, and—the nicest part, perhaps, if not the most essential—becoming best friends with each other, and with us.

The wisdom I've gained is transferable. You can read this book and learn what I've learned. The insights on the following pages can help you create a strong, healthy, loving family unit just as, by God's grace, they helped me create mine.

From each section I've extracted a principle—I'm calling it a "lesson"—to focus your attention on a possibly helpful insight that the particular passage is making. As you read, try to internalize the lessons that seem valuable to you. Check out what I was doing about the insight in the associated passage, and then figure out how you might incorporate the particular principle into your own family.

Chapter 1

Laying the Foundation for Parenthood

THE FIRST TWO YEARS OF OUR MARRIAGE were some of the toughest and yet best years of our lives.

One day early in my marriage I had an emotional breakdown in a store over eight cents worth of soup. A method we used of stretching our food dollars in those days was to buy cans of Campbell's Chicken Noodle Soup—four for a buck. On this particular day, however, I discovered that the grocery store had raised the price of that soup to 27 cents a can. I got all teary-eyed and my husband asked me, "Honey, what's wrong?"

"Oh, Alan!" I wailed, "we're going to starve!"

We were the quintessential starving students and trying to make it from paycheck-to-paycheck on a budget that was stretched as tight as the skin of a drum.

☆ 1

Begin Your Family with Your Marriage

FAMILY LIFE BEGINS WITH A MARRIAGE. The first step Alan and I took in raising children was preparing ourselves to be ready to receive them. The two of us went through a lot of experiences and changes before the advent of our first child, but the anticipation of someday bringing children into the world and raising them to become fulfilled human beings lay behind everything we did as a young couple. In a very real sense, one of our main goals in those early years was to prepare ourselves for parenthood.

I was born the fifth in a family of six children with four older brothers and a younger sister. Since I was raised in a large family I had learned household management, grocery shopping, and laundry. So, when I got married I was ready for marriage, as far as anyone can be said to be ready for that perilous adventure, even though I was only 17 years old at the time.

My 20-year-old fiancé, Alan, had just completed his first two years of college and was moving to Fresno to attend Fresno State University. It was important to us that we be married because we were desperately in love and couldn't face the agonies of separation.

Marriage was also important because we believed in our hearts that Heaven had brought the two of us together. We had met in church when I was 10 and Alan was 13. Ours was not a case of love at first sight. Far from it! At age 10 I had the opinion that all boys were gross in general and Alan was gross in particular.

We became friends as we participated in the church's youth group, and eventually became a couple.

At the beginning, our dates were conducted within the

context of group social events. Even though we were young, Alan and I were people of faith who had grown up worshipping and praying together. For whatever reason, unlike so many young people who are raised in church, we internalized the lessons and sermons we were hearing and began including prayer and Bible study as a couple from our first times together. The shared faith we had in common served to cement a strong bond between us.

It is important to secure the blessings of parents on any marriage union. As we moved from friendship to affection and then to romance, I had little trouble with my folks over the fact that I was in such a serious relationship with Alan at such a young age because from the beginning, my folks loved Alan too. They knew him to be a young man who had serious plans for his future. Alan's folks, however, were a little more cautious about the developing relationship because they knew that my approach to life was much less serious than Alan's.

His parents were right to have misgivings about me because in those days I was like a goose that wakes up every day to a new world—because she's forgotten everything that happened in the past. I was like the character Maria in *The Sound of Music* when she was a novice in the convent because I also was a cloud that couldn't be pinned down. I was a flibbertigibbet, will-o'-the wisp, and a clown.

☆ 2

Learn From the Tensions with Your Spouse

IT WOULD HAVE BEEN A TRAGEDY if either of us had married someone who was just like ourselves. We completed each other. The fact is that my impetuous nature served as a good foil for Alan's highly disciplined, organized, and reserved approach to life. He was good for me; I was good for him. He settled me down; I got him up on his feet and moving.

They talk about two people becoming one in marriage and that certainly was our experience because we came together to make a balanced whole. One of the great things that I've seen happen in my life is how I've developed and changed through the influence of my husband. For example, I still have great fun in my life but have come to understand that a disciplined life can be far more pleasurable than a life spent just doing whatever comes to mind. I came to see that by staying focused I actually had more time to play.

We all wake up in the morning with a list—whether written or unwritten—of things that we need to accomplish during the day. I learned that if I will only get to work, attack the list, finish it up, then I will have the rest of my time for fun and play.

On the other hand, if I do things randomly and helter-skelter, I spend the whole day with the darned list hanging over my head and will probably end up going to bed and sleeping uneasily because of the things I didn't get done that I really needed to do.

Alan and I got married in a beautiful wedding at our church. We had no idea what we were getting into—at that point nobody does—but we figured the Creator of the Universe—who brought this beautiful world out of nothing—could bring something fine out of the lives of two young people who were ignorant but passionately committed to finding His will. I like to imagine that, not counting the preacher, three of us were at the altar that day.

★ 3

Seek Independence from Your Parents

WHEN WE SAID, "I DO!" we meant that we were going to do it on our own without relying on anybody but God to carry us through. We had little money and few possessions. However, from the beginning, Alan and I both had a do-it-ourselves attitude.

We were determined never to go to our folks for the help that they would have been glad to supply.

It is important, I believe, for a young couple to sever the strings of dependency with their parents as soon as they are able to do so. The day we married Alan and I took complete responsibility for our finances. We moved to a tiny off-campus one-bedroom, half-bath apartment in Fresno, tightened our belts, enrolled in school, and got to work.

We were both going to school full-time—I was only in my junior year of high school. Plus we both got full-time jobs at two different Taco Bells. Alan was working the Taco Bell nightshift, I was working afternoons, and there were some periods when it seemed that our paths scarcely crossed. This was long before cell phones; I think we might have invented sticky notes, because we would leave these everywhere for each other as a way of keeping in touch.

The furious pace of our lives was compounded when we became involved in a church-planting mission in nearby Clovis that has since grown into a thriving church. Alan and I were soon sponsoring a Junior Chapel for children in the American Legion building, which the mission was renting at the time. We actually conducted our Junior Chapel crowded together into the tiny women's lounge of that building. We made the best of it. The kids didn't care about the cramped quarters; they simply loved being together and we loved being with them.

Alan also became the music director and started the mission's first choir.

Throughout every part of our lives we felt that we were being led hand-in-hand by God. Alan and I continued praying and studying the Bible together as a couple. During some periods we were too busy to keep that up, but those were the times when we struggled the most with our marriage.

☆ 4

Practice Creative Financial Responsibility

WE WERE LIVING HAND-TO-MOUTH lives but God was good. So were His people. Members of the mission would take us out to Sunday dinner and give us bags of food. Our needs were always supplied.

My husband was studying to become an accountant so he met head-on the financial challenges of tracking the budget and balancing our expenses with our incomes.

Our combined salaries from Taco Bell were insufficient to raise our standard of living to the Federal poverty level. Both incomes together seemed more like an allowance than an actual earnings. We went home one Christmas break and Alan spent two weeks working as a taper in his dad's sheetrock business and during that time earned more money than he and I had together made working full-time at Taco Bell from September to December.

Alan devised a perfect system to stretch our few dollars as far as possible. When we got our paltry Taco Bell pay each week he would put the money into a set of envelopes. Our tithe went into the first envelope. He then put money into other envelopes marked RENT, FOOD, GAS, LAUNDRY, and SAVINGS. Whatever was left over would go into the final envelope, labeled RECREATION. We usually put from $1 to $1.75 a week into that envelope.

It was a good system—and one that Alan has since been teaching to young adults all over the state. They often tell us later that they can't believe how good it works.

Everything we did was on a budget because the only plastic we had were Ziplocs; we had no credit to lure us into debt. If we couldn't afford to pay for something, we just went without it.

Air-conditioning was one big expense we could cut down on. We lived across the street from a large lawn owned by Fresno State. It didn't take us long to learn the schedule for the sprinkler system. So on insufferably hot days we would put on our shorts and run through the sprinklers, rather than waste money sitting in front of the air-conditioner. The sprinklers would cool us down without costing a dime. And running through sprinklers was a lot more fun than sitting in the blast of an air-conditioning unit.

We didn't have much money left over for recreation, but our needs in that area were even smaller than the resources.

When we got married Alan's folks gave us a Monopoly game. We had a good laugh when we opened the present, but in Fresno we spent a lot of time playing Monopoly together. We constructed a coffee table out of a wooden plank stretched across two orange crates that we had retrieved from the discard pile at our local grocery store.

We sanded that plank, varnished it, and then set the Monopoly game up on it. We never had enough time to play a complete game at a sitting so we left the thing set up all the time. We left the board, deeds, pieces, and money lying out. We would schedule playtime— an hour here and a half-hour there. A single game might take weeks to finish. As soon as one of us would go bankrupt we would set the game up again. We loved it!

Some days we scarcely had two nickels to rub together but in the game I might have Boardwalk loaded with hotels and if Alan's little silver shoe landed on my property, I had a sudden infusion of wealth that was delightful even if it was only virtual.

Our big date out was usually one of the dollar movies that Fresno State used to show in their open-air amphitheater. We would pay our dollar, spread out our sleeping bag, and watch a movie that might have been old when our folks were young. We loved those times together.

We didn't spend any money on greeting cards for each other. On some occasions such as a birthday, Valentine's Day, or Christmas we would go to the grocery store together, go to the greeting card aisle, and then read to each other the messages from the cards. We set a time limit and when our time was up we would say, "If I had money, this is the card I would buy you." Then we would take turns reading the particular card we had selected to the other.

It was a silly thing to do—but so much fun! Reading grocery store greeting cards to each other became a family tradition; we still do that sometimes. Of course, we could now buy all the cards we wanted, but the little ritual is a periodic reminder of where we came from.

The fact is, you can't really comprehend how blessed you are until you can see how far you have come. Those greeting cards make us laugh, and help us communicate how much we love each other, but they also mark for us how far God has brought us down the road since we were a young couple together.

Anyway, how nice is it to have your spouse actually read to you a Valentine's poem about love, or a birthday verse about how important you are?

ELIZABETH MAULDIN

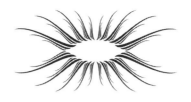

Chapter 2

Days of Preparation

THINGS WEREN'T ALWAYS EASY, but pressure was from the outside trying to come in. The two of us were on a course that God had put our feet on and it has always worked. We had morning and evening services on Sunday, with choir practice following the evening service, plus mid-week services every Thursday.

We were leading busy lives but we always reserved Sundays and Thursday evenings for God and for ourselves. We sometimes turned down opportunities to work during those times. We really could have used the extra money, but those set-aside times did a perfect job of demonstrating our conviction that money didn't come first.

There's a difference between commitment and conviction. A commitment is a promise that can be broken. Deep-rooted convictions cannot be changed. We have a conviction that God is the Master of our lives; in that context our relationship with each other always works out fine. Our spiritual convictions keep us from breaking our commitment to each other. It's a quality that a lot of couples miss.

☆ 5

Practice Parenting with Pets

AT ONE POINT WE SPENT SEVERAL months during which we were so busy that we didn't have time to spend the money in our recreation envelope. We found to our amazement that we had actually accrued the heady sum of $27.50 of mad money. We felt rich! We couldn't think of what to do with all that wealth.

The next day was Sunday and we were invited for lunch at the home of a couple who raised cocker spaniel puppies. They showed us the runt from a litter that they didn't know what to do with. We instantly fell in love with little Shiloh. When they saw how much we loved that little doggie they sold it to us for $27.50, even though it was much more valuable than that. The transaction represented a real sacrifice on their part, but a happy acquisition for us.

Little Shiloh was a buff-colored bundle of energy; beloved by everyone he met. Dogs are a constant expense but the people in the mission understood how important Shiloh was to us, and after that we would often find bags of dog food sitting beside the human food that those anonymous angels would leave for us.

Even worse than the expense, we discovered that the apartment complex had a rule against dogs. We were never able to leave him home alone, but the neighbors all fell in love with our little puppy and would take turns dog-sitting for us while we were at school or at work. We believed that God was with us and ensuring that everything was taken care of on our behalf—even providing dog-sitting services when we needed them.

Shiloh was amazing! Dogs in this breed are not notably intelligent but for some reason Shiloh apparently had an emotional sensitivity IQ that must have been over 150, because he moved in on hurting people with comfort.

Six months after we got him I had a miscarriage. We were crushed but that dog stayed by me during the entire time of my recovery—not simply staying by my side through my physical recovery, but remaining with me until I was finally over the emotional trauma.

Whenever we would grow stressed by circumstances, our little dog would sense the pressure that was weighing on our spirits and would move in on our need with all the doggie compassion and comfort that he was cable of giving.

The dog also had a highly developed sense of who was in the right in any argument or dispute and would curl up at the feet of the one that he deemed, in some mysterious fashion, to be the innocent party, while completely ignoring the other. We called him our Wrong Meter and pretended that he infallibly sensed who was erring.

One Thursday I was stuck in traffic and came home late. "Geri, we're going to be late! Hurry up!" Alan hollered at me. He continued hounding and badgering me as I struggled to get showered, changed, and to put my makeup on. I was just finishing up, standing there holding a tube of hand lotion when he said once more, "Geri, we have to get going!"

I swung around with that tube of lotion in my hand and, without meaning to (I think), but with a gesture as smooth as anything I ever did in my life, I squeezed the tube and sprayed the mark of Zorro right across his face.

As soon as I did that, with a deliberate and meaningful gesture little Shiloh plopped right down at my feet. Alan didn't say anything for a long moment. At last he recovered from his shock and finally asked, "Do you feel better?"

"I think we both feel better," I answered. "Don't we, Shiloh?"

Alan really was a great sport at such times. He never batted an eye, but just wiped off the lotion. In the following days we would laugh about that event every time something brought the memory to our minds. I'm still laughing.

That's the way our arguments went. Brief tempests that always ended in restoration of peace and usually in laughter.

I'm a woman full of sand and vinegar and Alan and I have our disagreements, but they are always brief; we always come back together again. The contention we are arguing about is of no consequence when compared to the beautiful thing that binds us together. Our marriage has a strong foundation because it is built on a sense of purpose.

☆ 6

Hang on During Difficult Times

WHEN WE GOT MARRIED A NUMBER of friends and even family members confidently predicted that I would quit school before long, but I was determined to finish my studies. My grades as a married woman were actually higher than when I was single. Not long after I enrolled in the Fresno school I got a 'D' in a class and was forced to take the grade report home to get it signed.

It is embarrassing to take a 'D' home to your parents to sign, but it is a really bitter pill to swallow when you have to take the grade report home to be signed by your husband! It became a defining moment; the humiliation changed my life! I resolved that there would be no second occurrence. From that point on I was on the honor roll.

The fact is that I only made it through school and we only made it financially because of a series of tragedies.

During those two years I experienced three miscarriages. At the time every one of them seemed an incredible loss, but I believe that God works things out just as we would have chosen them ourselves if we could see The Big Picture from His viewpoint.

Those miscarriages were early events through which I learned the lesson that we can't always understand what God is doing. Understanding is never required of me nor is it often given to me. What is required is that I come to believe that He knows what He's doing even when I don't know; he's working out His plan even when I can't see the plan.

I've come to believe that as long as I stay the course, the course will always get easier. Also, I've come to believe that sometimes the things we go through aren't for our sake, but for the sake of those who are watching our response.

I might have gotten some insight about my lost babies.... I have come to believe that I lost those earlier ones because God had ordained that I should have the four children that I eventually gave birth to, and the fifth that we adopted. I can't imagine any one of them not having come into my life.

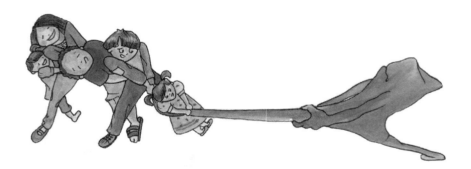

☆ 7

Work Through Your Failures

TWO YEARS AFTER OUR WEDDING we graduated from school in ceremonies that were separated by only a week. But shortly before our graduation ceremonies I experienced a collapse of confidence in God's faithfulness and in my husband's wisdom that was as shameful as it was unexpected.

The week of graduation, the mission threw us a huge farewell party. There was a lot of laughter and tears, and I was suddenly struck by a terrible conviction that we were about to leave behind the only resources that would ever be able to make us happy. It seemed to me that whatever waited for us in the murky future ahead would be completely incapable of replacing the roots we had put down during our two years together in that place.

For some reason, I became certain that the home we had made with each other, the friendships we had formed, and the ministries that we had found would be lost forever and nothing would ever be right in our lives again. I was overwhelmed to the point of incapacity by the sense that I was about to be pulled away from everything that would ever be able to give my life structure, purpose, and most of all, security.

I told Alan with a real sense of anguish, "I don't know if I can do this." He kept reassuring me that it would be OK but I didn't believe him. In my frightened confusion I left him and went to spend some time with friends in hopes that I could recover my equilibrium and summon sufficient energy to move on to the next stage of my life.

Fortunately, when I flew away from my husband to seek some

refuge from the storm, a pastor friend of mine was the person to whom I flew. After a couple days the search for my missing resolve came to an abrupt end when the pastor looked at me and asked, "Geraldine, where is God in all this?"

It was the right question asked at the right moment because I was stopped in my tracks by the realization that God wasn't to be found anywhere in my flying away and flailing around.

I began to weep. My attitude changed in that moment. My fears evaporated when by an act of faith that was as deliberate as it was simple, I returned God to His place in my thinking and philosophy. The pastor held me for a moment and then asked, "Would you like me to take you home?"

"Yes!"

☆ 8

Learn the Ways of Repentance and Reconciliation

MY FEARS CONCERNING THE FUTURE were now replaced by a sense of terrible regret over the pain that my loss of faith had inflicted upon Alan. My incomprehensible failure had marred a time that should have been full of celebration, happiness, and joyful expectation, deforming it into a dark period of doubt, confusion, and even abandonment.

My remorse over the hurt that I had caused my husband became, if anything, a source of even greater pain for me than the internal conflict that had driven me away. I would have done anything to undo the harm that I had caused, but there was nothing to be done apart from tearfully seeking Alan's forgiveness.

Of course, being the man that he is, Alan forgave me instantly from his heart without a word of reproach. I think it was easier—far easier, in fact—for Alan to forgive me for my lapse of confidence than it was for me to forgive myself.

I can imagine that Alan was grateful for the fact that the cheerful, sunny, faithful woman he had married had resumed her place in his life—replacing the fearful, weepy, and insecure wench who, for a short time, had unaccountably taken her place.

My restoration became complete two days later when Alan graduated from Fresno State. Following the commencement ceremony I hugged him and the moment brought us a sense of accomplishment that has hardly ever been equaled in our lives since.

"We did it!"

It wasn't easy—quite the opposite. But we had seen the

thing through to the end. Nothing in the decades that have passed since then have served to shine any light upon the cause of that mysterious failure of nerve that had so suddenly and completely overtaken me. The incident came down to a failure of confidence on my part. I didn't trust my husband's plan for our lives. But the even more awful failure was in not trusting in God's plan.

Someone recently showed me a great quote by the author Henry Miller:

> *Life moves on, whether we act as cowards or heroes. Life has no other discipline to impose, if we would but realize it, than to accept life unquestioningly.*

And then Miller added a shining observation that I have found to be true through many experiences:

> *Everything we shut our eyes to, everything we run away from, everything we deny, denigrate or despise, serves to defeat us in the end. What seems nasty, painful, evil, can become a source of beauty, joy, and strength, if faced with an open mind. Every moment is a golden one for him who has the vision to recognize it as such.*

What happened to me in that awful experience was simply a failure of courage caused by a loss of vision. I understand what happened, but I'll never understand why it happened, since neither God nor my husband had ever given me a reason to doubt their faithfulness. I learned lessons from the experience, however, as Miller said people "with an open mind" would. But I still will not call that moment "a golden one."

☆ 9

Move on

ONE OF THE THINGS THAT SHOULD have reassured me during this time is that Alan always had a plan. He knew where he wanted to go in his life and knew how he wanted to get there. We moved back to our Northern California home where Alan began working two nearly full-time jobs—one in an office, so he could get some experience working in that type of environment, and the other working in his dad's business.

We used the cash from that not-to-be-touched SAVINGS envelope to put a down payment on a three-bedroom, bath-and-a-half home in Pittsburg, which is a 15-minute drive from where my family home was, in Martinez.

Alan began working for a Lafayette accounting firm. For a year he was miserable in that 9-to-5 job. He found his second job to be far more satisfying—working until 9 p.m. in his father's business.

He wanted the office experience that he could gain at the accounting firm, but loved working with his dad.

A year after moving to Pittsburg our first son was born. At the time some people wondered if it wasn't difficult for me to be carrying the baby while my husband was working those long hours, but the fact is that we never knew any other way of living. Our schedules had been full and running over like that since we had been married.

We had developed great skills in simply making good use of whatever little time we could squeeze in together.

I think we could derive more genuine satisfaction out of a

half-hour playing some silly game together or simply talking than some couples might take from a weekend away. Perhaps those moments we were with each other were made even more precious because the time was so fleeting. We never had the luxury of having enough time to come to the point where we could begin to take each other for granted.

Alan felt right at home working for his dad's company. When he was only 11 years old he had started working around the place after school and during vacations, doing things such as sweeping and moving supplies. His dad later converted the business to sheetrock and Alan started doing "scrap," which is the industry term for cleaning up the homes following a project. Later he was promoted to be a taper, and then learned the other parts of the business—doing mud, stuccoing, and texturing.

Alan would have been content to remain in the family business but his dad wanted him to go to school. He told him, "I don't want you living with regrets that you weren't able to go to college."

Chapter 3
Setting Foundational Principles

THE ROBUST FAMILY LIFE WE have enjoyed for the past decades was no accident; it came about through a number of principles that we as parents established for our children. One of these is the right of each family member to be their own person and find their own unique way through life. When the children were young there were portents of the destinies that awaited them.

When my first two sons were still young I once walked by the bathroom and saw four-year-old Brian had his two-year-old brother Matthew folded up and sitting Indian style inside the toilet.

"What are you doing?" I asked Brian.

"I'm baptizing Matthew," he said.

I had a hard time keeping from laughing right out loud. One of my most rigid principles of discipline with my children has been never to laugh at them when they are being serious, since that is always a demeaning thing to do to a child.

Sometimes, like at that particular moment, keeping a straight face was painful.

In a restrained voice I said to Brian, "When Matthew gets ready to be baptized, he'll get baptized then." It was difficult to make the point that Matthew wasn't ready for baptism because he was obviously having the time of his life sitting there sloshing around in the toilet bowl.

I can also remember Brian lining up his siblings and neighborhood friends in the backyard and preaching to them. They loved to play church together!

When Matthew was little he always paid attention to music and has developed himself as a musician. Brittany was a charmer who would light up a room when she walked into it. Malia was the quiet observer and animal lover. In retrospect, it seemed that childhood experiences and predilections became harbingers for the lives that the children would eventually come to lead, because Brian is attending Western Seminary in Sacramento. Matthew works with sound systems and does musical performances. Brittany is the head of our church nursery. And Malia is studying to be a veterinarian technician.

☆ 10

Cherish Diversity

I ALWAYS TRIED TO BE CAREFUL WITH expectations for our children when they were young. The fact is, we never wanted to exert any control over the character of the destiny that waited for each of our children. The lack of expectations worked well because it gave the kids room to breathe, leaving them free to explore the world and their own character, and to discover for themselves whatever purpose they could find for their lives.

We never wanted the kids to be like us or to be like each other. We raised five people to be individuals, and now four of them are married to other individuals. We could have adopted the cable station USA's tagline as our own: "Characters welcome." One of the qualities that makes our family the happy unit that it has become is that we appreciate and even celebrate the differences among ourselves.

The individuality that marks the lives of our family members and that sets us off from each other had its roots in my relationship to my husband. From the beginning of our times together, we acknowledged that we were completely—often laughably—different from each other; we made our differences work out by creating synergisms that caused our marriage to function so beautifully.

So now I am blessed with grown children, each of whom is complete in themselves to an amazing degree—the result of conscious, determined effort, of "pantyhose parenting." And the children now have brought spouses into the family circle, which all serve to bring unique qualities and tastes of their own into the family blend, and adding even more fuel to fan the flames of love that are burning among us.

A standard of mutual love and affection is another foundational principle in our family. We have our moments, of course, when we have disagreements and sometimes we might not even like each other a lot. But we all love each other passionately and forever.

One of my greatest satisfactions is that we didn't raise perfect children, but raised them to love each other, love their parents, and love God above all else. We don't demand perfection; the children don't have to be perfect as long as they strive to do what's right.

☆ 11

Leverage Imperfection

ONE DANGER WE'VE AVOIDED IS ANY arrogant refusal to admit our own errors and shortcomings. Alan and I have made plenty of mistakes and have always admitted to our kids that we are not perfect. Sometimes we have to ask our kids to forgive us.

The fact is that when we parents show some bad judgment or have lost our temper, we really do need to seek forgiveness. Just as importantly, our kids need to learn to forgive.

Forgiving and being forgiven are the essential parts of an act of total restoration. The world is full of dysfunctional families because family members never learned to sincerely apologize—never earnestly asked for and received forgiveness. So the wounds that they had naturally inflicted upon each other were allowed to fester.

Of course, it's humiliating to have to ask my kid to forgive me, but what better basis can parents have for expecting children to be contrite about bad behavior than by modeling contrition ourselves?

Perhaps as important as modeling the behavior, the act of seeking forgiveness is an essential part of integrity. Parents who can never bring themselves to admit they are wrong, then apologize and seek forgiveness, are merely pretending to be above any wrong-hearted, wrong-headed, or simply mistaken act. They aren't fooling anybody. The kids know the truth, so hypocrisy becomes the actual behavior we end up modeling for them. "Values are caught not taught," they say, and the kids quickly learn to disguise their own faults or excuse away their own errors and misbehaviors. We've shown them how to do that.

By being honest and transparent in front of our children, we are, in fact, able to use the honest admission of our own errors as a basis for accepting our kids when they screw up. The kids know they need to apologize because they've seen us apologize. They know that we will forgive them because they forgave us.

The social skills and the grace that accompany the acts of seeking, granting, and receiving forgiveness are some of the most important lessons you can teach your child. Forgiven people forgive people. Acts of giving and receiving forgiveness are more than simply learned behaviors, but they are certainly behaviors that we get better at with practice.

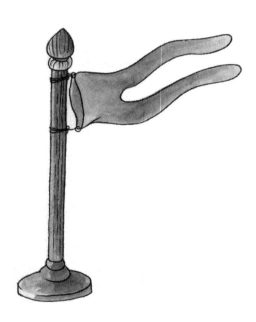

☆ 12

Let Go of the Kids When it Is Time to Do So

AS THE CHILDREN GREW OLDER, another foundational principle we established was to let them go. We are responsible *to* our grown children but are not responsible *for* them. It's a big distinction. Once the kids married and moved out, Alan and I continued to love them as much as ever but, thank God, we were no longer required to be responsible for their actions and decisions. We still provide whatever help is appropriate, and give them advice whenever they come to us for advice, but when they moved out of our house they became responsible for themselves.

That freedom from responsibility has become a liberating thing in my own life. It's great when the kids come and ask for advice. Sometimes when they ask me what they should do, I tell them, "Advice is like armpits. Everyone has some but they usually stink." But then I try to give them whatever counsel I can.

They have learned the wisdom of surrounding themselves with people who care about making them a better person. And that company of trusted counselors includes Alan and me. We are free to say whatever we want because of the reality that they are perfectly free not to do what we say; we're not giving them instructions about how to run their lives.

Sometimes we might not say things they want to hear, but in some cases they need to hear it, and in any case they don't have to listen. If they follow our advice, however, they themselves must still bear the responsibility for whether the advice turns out to be good or bad.

Sometimes the kids take our advice, other times they don't.

Alan and I aren't emotionally affected either way because we know that it is their life, not ours. And they all know that we know. So there's no chance that the atmosphere will get heated, as would certainly be the case if we felt the need to try to control their lives or if they thought we were trying to exercise that kind of control.

For example, Matthew runs his own household, and we're glad to let him run it. Brian runs his household; our son-in-law, Dustin, runs his household. Sometimes they do things we don't agree with, but it is up to them to make their choices and to reap the reward for their decisions or to suffer the consequences.

☆ 13

Cherish In-laws

DURING ALL THEIR LIVES OUR CHILDREN, of course, have had disagreements with each other, and have come to Alan and me to be arbitrators. When they start to fuss at each other I try to be like Sergeant Friday, "I just want the facts, Ma'am!" and then offer some kind of opinion without actually taking sides.

Now that the kids are getting married, I find my standard of impartiality breaking down sometimes because we are often prone to pick the in-law side in a disagreement. And the kids accept it; they realize what is happening.

I never understood why mothers-in-law sometimes do things to make the people their kids have married feel like outsiders. How significant is it to me, and to the health of our whole family, that a daughter-in-law or a son-in-law feel like she or he belongs in the inner Mauldin circle?

That sense of belonging is a very important, if not essential, part of any successful marriage. I'm going to love with all my heart the people my kids marry and do whatever I can to make myself loveable to them. After all, I loved my in-laws almost as much as I loved Alan's in-laws. And they came to love me as they loved him. I think that that shared love played an important role in the love that Alan and I have for each other.

☆ 14

Practice the Golden Rule, and More

GIVING GROWN CHILDREN THE FREEDOM to make their way through life without our interference as parents is simply one of those Golden Rule things since, after all, my husband and I have our own lives to live and never wanted anybody telling us how to live it.

We parents can cut out a lot of nonsense if we simply make it an inflexible principle to practice the Golden Rule with our kids during every part of our relationship with them. Imagine how that might impact our behavior. We don't like people screaming at us. We don't like people not showing us respect, or criticizing us, or ignoring us, or talking mean to us, or calling us stupid, or hitting us....

If we could just learn to put ourselves in our children's shoes and become deliberately and habitually empathetic with them— continually asking ourselves, "How would I feel at this moment if I were my child and somebody was treating me the way I'm treating him or her?" then some of us would engage in instantly transformed parental behaviors.

I believe that a lot of children grow up angry and resentful of their parents simply because the parents never tried to imagine the effect that their attitudes and behaviors were having on their children.

For the most part, our relationship with our children should be more than a Golden Rule. There's a so-called Platinum Rule that tells us, "Do unto others what others want you to do to them."

During some phases of childhood the Platinum Rule would

be unworkable since, of course, you aren't going to let them do things like play in the street when they are four or go to an unsupervised all-nighter when they are 14, no matter how much they plead and beg. But for the most part, we should get in the habit of living by the Platinum Rule. Don't give the kids a Sandy Patti or Merle Haggard CD if they want to listen to Flight Of The Conchords or Nickelback.

Be careful playing the "THIS IS GOOD FOR YOU" card.

☆ 15

Learn the Power of Responsible Behavior

A MAJOR FOUNDATIONAL PRINCIPLE in our family was giving and accepting of responsibility. Our message to our children was that they must be responsible for their own choices. We helped them become aware that there are consequences from the choices they make. Whether it's concerning a member of their family now, or friends and coworkers at some time in the future, they had to prepare themselves to accept the consequences that follow from the things they chose to do.

Even when our kids were young we tried to make them responsible for the consequences of their behaviors.

Doing so permitted us to impose soft guidelines on the children rather than enforcing rigid rules. The difference between the two is that guidelines are based on rationalized causes and effects; rules, on the other hand, are based on the mere exercise of authority.

As they grew older, not only did our children learn what behaviors were expected of them and forbidden to them, but they always understood the moral and ethical context of the standard we were imposing at each point.

One way we accomplished this was to avoid using the phrase "Because I said so, that's why!" Some parents imagine that their children, especially when very young, aren't able to understand the reasons why some behaviors are required while others are forbidden, but the fact is, even young children can understand moral reasoning.

You can always find a way to describe why a thing is right

or wrong—required or forbidden. Doing so gives you the ability to help you base discipline on values rather than merely on the threat of punishment.

I learned of a sheriff in a small town in Michigan who gave his teenage boy a new pickup. Before they had made the first payment, the boy was driving recklessly and totaled the pickup completely. The officer who made out the traffic report said to the sheriff, "What do you want me to do about your son?"

The sheriff answered, "If you don't give that kid a ticket, I'll give him one myself."

Bold answer! The boy had to pay his fine and work off the debt for the pickup. But the kid said later that it was one of the best things that ever happened to him. It changed him completely. His school marks improved, his attitude at home improved, and he developed a new seriousness toward life.

Assuming this kind of moral control over one's life becomes a big part of becoming mature and responsible adults. Children learn that they can't have it both ways. They must assume ownership of their actions, whether good or bad. That way they learn not to blame behaviors on their parents, their upbringing, their teachers, the size of their bank account, or spiritual influences in their lives.

A young boy once drew all over the dining room wall with crayons. "Why did you do that?" his mother asked.

"The Devil made me do it."

So the mother grabbed the boy and gave him a spanking. After he calmed down she gave him a second spanking. "Why did you spank me two times?" the boy wailed.

"Well, the first time I spanked you for drawing on the wall with crayons," she said. "The second time I spanked you for listening to the Devil."

I never would have given the child a whipping, let alone two whippings but the story is a good illustration of the principle of forcing children to assume responsibility for their actions.

The Devil or any other force on the face of the planet cannot make us do anything against a determined will; we make our own choices. We are without excuse.

We taught our children to be moral decision-makers by giving them freedom over whether or not they would stay within the lines of our standards and values. In that way they were able to reap both the rewards and the penalties of their actions. They could grasp in their hearts the principle that doing a good job or good deed earned a reward. Crossing the line and screwing up in some way earned a punishment. The child could accept responsibility for the good outcomes as well as for the bad ones because they had control over the process in either case.

☆ 16

Practice Responsible Behavior

IT'S EASY TO HANDLE KIDS WHEN they are acting like kids, but it is much more difficult dealing with parents who are acting childish. We work with a lot of self-absorbed young people and when you look at their parents, you see the source from which the youngsters derived the "all about me" life principle they are operating under.

People can be brought back from the awful effects of bad home environments, but the most efficient way of changing people is to make the change on the level of the family, and that means helping parents assume responsibility for the children they brought into the world.

They used to say that "Charity begins at home," but the fact is, a lot of things begin at home. Some modern parents seem to be ready to pass blame on to schools, churches, the media, society, and religious institutions rather than take responsibility for the impact that their own roles as parents have had on their children.

When things go wrong such parents lash out at anybody but themselves. That kind of behavior is so deadly to any kind of intervention because as long as parents refuse to accept the responsibility for whatever problem their child is having, they thwart any effective remedy on their part. Clearly if the parents have no fault in a matter, neither are they responsible to do something to fix the problem.

There's a part in every human being, including me, that wishes they could obey a list of rules and be spared the onus of making choices that will control their life. We have all met people who profess to be good, but live lives that are diminished and constrained by the list of things they must avoid and that other list of the things they must do. They are proving the wisdom of Thoreau when he said, "Any fool can make a rule, and any fool will mind it."

It's easy for parents to say that they want to raise children who will become responsible adults—equipped by attitudes and spiritual resources to take charge of their lives. But it is more difficult to avoid making decisions for children, rather than letting them make their own decisions and then allowing them to experience the positive or negative consequences of their choices. It is easy to make excuses for children and to shelter them from expressing themselves as individuals and accepting the consequences for their actions.

Effective child rearing comes with associated costs that parents often try to avoid. It is easier to do a kid's homework for him than to help him do it himself. It is easier to impose our will upon children rather than letting a child make a decision about clothes or use of time and then to coach them about the benefits or costs of the decision.

☆ 17

Make Wise Use of Technology

ANOTHER FOUNDATIONAL PRINCIPLE is to guide and monitor how children use their time.

Parents blame the technology for what the technology is doing to the life of the family, but the fact is that we've copped out on our responsibilities by using the technology to keep our kids out of our faces and out of our hair.

Television has made it much easier to take care of kids at home. When they are younger we stick them in front of the TV as a way of making our lives easier. But as they grow older our lives become tougher, because the technology that was such a good babysitter for our children when they were young has created a communication barrier now that they are older. Kids today spend too much time texting each other, cell phoning each other, surfing the Internet, watching TV, and sitting or walking around with their iPod earbuds stuck in their ears. They are both connected, and cut off.

We always imposed guidelines for things such as television viewing. We created a structure for the children's daily lives that allowed technology to come in as a tool but never as a master. Lacking that sense of structure has lured many modern children into living an *ad hoc* existence, merely doing what feels good to them even when what feels good *to* them often turns out to be not good *for* them.

☆ 18

Promote Positive Attitudes

WE ALSO OPERATED ON THE relative importance of attitudes over behavior. In many cases we were faced with the necessity of making an attitude adjustment rather than merely correcting an action. Almost every issue in life comes down to attitude because, as someone pointed out, "When you change the way you look at things, the things you look at change."

For all parents the attitude-adjustment process begins with themselves. We must provide for our children an example of the kind of person they should become. As far as I know nobody ever talks about child rearing as a type of mentorship, but that's just what it is. Our kids model themselves after us, whether we like it or not. Kids raised by loving people become loving people. Kids raised by drunkards become alcoholics.

We've got to bring home to ourselves the lessons we want our kids to learn. We must develop within ourselves the values of love, integrity, peacefulness, kindness, faithfulness, and self-control that we hope will be found in them.

☆ 19

Lead Grace-filled and Love-filled Lives

ANOTHER IMPORTANT FOUNDATIONAL PRINCIPLE in our family is the acknowledgement of the importance of grace. Someone once said that marriage destroys more good friendships than any other social institution. I think that's often the case, but our marriage has been supported by an energy from outside our relationship.

In my upbringing, we girls were taught not to marry anyone who isn't a Christian. But there's something much more important than that; it is desperately important to avoid a romantic entanglement with any person who is not on a path of spiritual growth.

Even more important than choosing a spouse with this characteristic is the importance of getting on—and remaining on—that track of spiritual growth ourselves. If a man or woman is not growing in the qualities of the spirit—such as servanthood, kindness, peacefulness, and faithfulness—then he or she will make a poor spouse and an even poorer parent. Alan and I couldn't have made it together without a lot of prayer. But we've done a lot of praying. The things of the spirit have always been important to us.

Some days we have had disagreements, but there has never been a day, or even an instant, when we considered leaving each other. "For better or for worse" is the standard and the pledge. You are forced to work through that "worse" when there is no Plan B. "I've never considered divorcing my husband for a single moment," said the wife of one prominent Christian leader. "I've thought about shooting him a few times."

Someone said, "The best gift you can give to your children is to love their mother." I think that's true, but there's a companion to that. One of the best things a husband can do for his wife is to love her children. The absentee father is a growing phenomenon and one that is sowing seeds that will yield a bitter harvest in the lives of the children who have been abandoned by their dads.

The most basic foundational principle that Alan and I created for our family was this love that the two of us had for each other. The greatest source of stability and serenity in our home has always come from the fact that I'm a one-man woman married to a one-woman man. We've always been good with each other. We're not perfect, but that's what makes us perfect for each other. We are best buddies; we fell into friendship a long time before we fell into love.

☆ 20

Earn Respect from Intention-based Living

ANOTHER IMPORTANT FOUNDATIONAL PRINCIPLE for our family is to focus attention on intention. We try to identify motives that lie behind behaviors and choices. Alan and I haven't been flawless, but our intentions have always been perfect. We have a perfect desire to be for each other what the other person needs. Our intentions for our children have also been to be the kind of parents they need us to be. We work at this. We labor over it. Every day we try to get this right.

The most powerful part of intention is when it is brought to bear on love. We should love each other passionately, but also learn to love each other deliberately. Love is certainly something you feel but more importantly it is something you do. True love becomes a choice—a deliberate movement of the will.

Alan is a grounded Christian, a God-fearing man. Our children don't merely love their father, they respect him and value their dad's friendship.

Alan is a man of uncompromising integrity. The men who work with and for Alan respect him. He's a nice guy as well as being a good man. The kids he has coached, as well as their parents, also respect him. Over the course of a year, Alan and I might receive 30 or 40 cards from kids he's dealt with who are still seeking advice from us.

We are supposed to respect our husbands, but Alan has earned my respect. Children are supposed to respect their parents, but Alan and I have earned our children's respect.

☆ 21

Work on Your Marriage

OUR MARRIAGE IS ONE OF THE STRONGEST foundational principles in our family. That didn't happen by accident.

Every marriage is a garden because it is a vibrant resource that can provide an unending supply of things such as emotional support, sexual pleasures, happiness, boundless good humor, comfort, and self-assurance—all those important qualities that can strengthen us and equip us to face the world outside of the marriage with confidence and hope.

But because a marriage is like a garden, it also requires a great deal of work and attention. We've all seen far too many cases in which a young couple stand together at the altar with the garden plot of their lives together before them. The rows are all nicely laid out, manicured and beautiful, waiting for the couple to supply the sunshine of love, fondness, and affection together with the life-giving water of respect and honor that will grow the seeds of the relationship that they planted during their courtship until they reap an amazing harvest of communion and love.

Integrity, honest confession, and heartfelt forgiveness are waiting as tools with which the couple can attack every day the weeds of mistrust, betrayal, and indifference that are bound to spring up, constantly trying to choke out the beautiful qualities that the couple is hoping to grow there.

But then what happens? The couple soon grows lazy and indifferent about the garden. They begin to ignore it and to foolishly imagine that the garden will take care of itself. Until one day they are shocked to discover that the garden of their marriage has, in fact, vanished beneath a wilderness of thorns, thistles, and ugly weeds.

The thing that was supposed to be beautiful has become disgusting to them and they finally get to the place where they can see no possibility more satisfying than simply burning the whole thing up through the flames of a bitter divorce.

It's a horrible picture, but one that is working itself out in failing marriages all around us. The couple is left confused and bewildered by the failure of their dreams. And they always imagine that the fault lies with some failure, great change, or "irreconcilable difference" of the other person when, in fact, the two of them simply failed to spend their time—sometimes on their knees and with sweat running off their foreheads—working together to keep the garden of their marriage fresh and alive.

"You only get out of a thing what you put into it" is a wise maxim that is more accurately said about a marriage than about any other thing on earth.

☆ 22

Practice Indomitable Love

TO HAVE A CLOSE-KNIT FAMILY IN today's society you have to be willing to go the distance. It never happens automatically. A family like ours, close and enjoying spending time together, has come about through deliberate and conscious choices that we have made and continue to make. We choose to live like this. We make a choice to like each other. It's another aspect of pantyhose parenting.

We're creating a strong family unit that was more common in previous decades than it is now. The Judds sang a great song "Tell me about the good old days," which asks the question:

Did lovers really fall in love to stay
And stand beside each other come what may?
Was a promise really something people kept
Not just something they would say?
Did families really bow their heads to pray?
Did daddies really never go away?
Oh, Grandpa, tell me 'bout the good old days

We moved backward to those "good old days" when it was OK to set aside a family night when you played cards, ate popcorn, or played hide-and-go-seek in the dark.

Alan and I have noted that the way we raised our children became foundations for the relationships that we enjoy with them as adults.

Having established this background describing the values that we hold to in our family, I want to go on and talk in some details about what I've learned about raising kids.

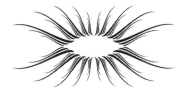

Chapter 4

Encouraging Virtues

THE MOST IMPORTANT TASK FOR any parent is to do everything possible in order to encourage their children to form good, positive relationships with others and to maintain high levels of goodness.

☆ 23

Create a Family Culture of Gratitude

WHEN OUR OLDEST CHILD, BRIAN, was about seven years old we began to encourage the keeping of a gratitude journal. Every evening before he went to bed he had to write down one thing that he was grateful for. When the other kids came along, they began doing that as well. Each night they had to write something, even if it was a short one-line entry.

When our youngest daughter, Malia—the animal lover—was six years old she caught a frog one day, put it in a box, and brought the box into the house. I told her that the frog would probably jump out of the box and that she should keep it outside. I guess my warning had made her nervous because the next day she wrote in her journal, "Thank you, God, for not letting my frog get out of the box."

Keeping a gratitude journal became a happy thing in our family because it forced the children every day into a recurring pattern of gratefulness that, I'm sure, marked their young lives. One unanticipated outcome of the exercise was that it made it easier for the children to talk to each other. When one of them did something good it was easier for a sibling to say, "That was a good thing you did," and have the other respond, "Thanks for saying that. I thought it was a good thing."

They had learned the language of gratitude. They had developed patterns of speech that made it natural to recognize something that they were grateful for and found it easy to express their thankfulness.

When you have a heart filled with gratitude there's no room for disgruntlement.

☆ 24

Enforce Family Peace

OUR KIDS WOULD FUSS AT EACH OTHER, though they did it less often than most siblings. We trained them to get along by forcing them to do so. As Brian and Matthew grew up together, those two boys loved each other. They were allowed to disagree and to argue, but were never allowed to fight with each other.

We had a firmly enforced house rule against fighting; violence was never an option. From the beginning we required our children to find peaceable ways to resolve disagreements.

The standard for harmony in our family involved more than simply banning the use of fists, elbows, and knees to get one's way, but forcing the children to actually resolve their differences, manage their anger, and find ways to get back into fellowship with the each other.

I always made it my deliberate goal to maintain the sense of harmony and peace that I believe to be the birthright of every child, and to ensure that such harmony was restored every time it was broken.

And that "every time" was our unyielding standard. The Bible tells us not to let the sun go down on our anger, and we worked steadily and deliberately to never let a day in our household end with unresolved conflicts.

We always enforced Moshe Dayan's principle that if you want to make peace, you don't talk to your friends. You talk to your enemies. In our household we made the kids talk through their periods of anger and enmity until they were once again peaceable and friendly with each other.

Conflict resolution begins in the nursery. Attitudes about ownership, territory, and entitlement begin to be set before a child learns to walk. Patterns of hostility and aggression can become so set in early childhood that for the rest of a person's life they will limit his or her ability to carry on healthy relationships.

Sometimes, of course, children will get over early conflicts; siblings can become good friends who were childhood enemies. But many times fighting children put into place patterns of hostility that families can never overcome no matter how costly the therapy they engage in as adults, or how many self-help books they read.

In later years too many families have difficult times when they are together and only endure events like Thanksgiving because of the desire to maintain family ties. But the celebration becomes filled with tension and poorly suppressed animosity. Everyone is relieved when the day is finally over for another year.

Those awful situations have been building through patterns of behavior that were being set in the family's earliest years. Siblings fighting with each other; parents fighting with each other; parents and siblings fighting with each other…. The family life becomes an endless series of competitions and struggles for power and supremacy. The children were raised with a sense of selfishness and entitlement that the family culture drilled into them. Getting the upper hand became like a matter of survival; if you didn't watch out for yourself, your family members would eat you up.

I saw how kids in some families are free to rip each other up. Family members never come to view the family unit as a God-given gift, but try to adapt the family to the patterns of the world that teach them to take care of themselves, to "watch out for number one," and to satisfy their own desires no matter the cost.

Alan and I have dealt with children who were absolutely out of control. They were lacking any boundaries for their actions and passions. They were choosing a path of self-destruction. Such situations have come about through a series of bad choices that the children were making, often because of bad choices their parents had made. As a result, decisions are always made solely on how an action will affect the decision-maker with no regard for the impact that the decision will have on others. The hugely dysfunctional reality of selfish patterns of behavior is that a purely selfish lifestyle imposes severe limitations on the ability of the individual to prosper as a human being.

All these out-of-control children are desperately unhappy. They have never learned the truth that Christ taught: "Give and it will be given unto you."

Parents are able to exert powerful influences upon their children, for both good and bad. We are able to nip dysfunctional behaviors in the bud if only we will leverage our influence in making positive change.

One day when Brian and Matt were eight and six, I walked into their room and heard them arguing over a Nintendo game. Matt was a chunky child. As so often happens with children (and adults) in this kind of situation, rather than arguing why it should be his turn, Brian made a personal attack on Matthew, slamming him about his weight.

I turned to Brian and instead of telling him that he should share, I knelt down on the floor so I could be on an eye-to-eye level with him—since the eyes speak more clearly than the voice—and told him, "I don't care whose turn it is you, don't talk to my son in that way!"

He got the message that I was taking this personally. He had crossed a line and had said something that had not only offended his brother—which was his purpose, of course—but he had also offended me. And he knew that wasn't a good idea.

☆ 25

Assign Time Together Rather than Time-out

I DIDN'T STOP THE INTERVENTION AT THE point of making Brian understand that he had offended me. One of the main roles that we have as parents is that of negotiator. We do a better job of parenting, I think, when we become mediators rather than umpires. We should try to bring our children together during times of dispute rather than trying to establish a demilitarized zone between them.

I wouldn't let my children be apart from each other when they were having difficulties. In the case of Brian and Matthew and the Nintendo game, I created an activity for the two of them that was designed to bring them back to a place of harmony and mutual affection. I took out two pieces of paper and two pencils. Then I set them down on the floor with them and I asked Matthew to write the 10 funniest things he could think of about Brian and Brian to write the 10 funniest things he could think of about Matthew. When they were finished they exchanged their lists and each read the 10 things about himself that the other brother had found most amusing. Long before they had finished reading their lists, the issue of whose turn it was on the Nintendo had vanished.

The few minutes of fun really did change them; after that I would hear things like, "I think it's my turn but it doesn't matter—you take another turn."

Our goal was not to be the best parents in the world, but to help our children be the best people they could possibly be. That meant that they had to learn to get along with their siblings. And that, in turn, meant they had to spend time with their siblings so that they would learn to get along.

Matt and Brittany had personal chemistries that caused them to spend the most time together because of all my children those two had the most difficulty relating to each other. Some of the problem might have been due to the fact that the two of them were only 18 months apart and were both at approximately the same point of development. Whatever the explanation, if one of them had something, the other always seemed to want it. The two of them were continually getting into fights and disagreements. Whenever they started arguing or fighting, I would bring them together and tell them to remain in each other's company until they worked things out.

When they were seven and eight they acted like the enforced time together was a death sentence. "Nooo!" they would scream. But they learned that they couldn't get out of it. This wasn't a "time-out"; it was a "time together." And I made it stick. If one of them had to go to the bathroom, the other had to stand in the hall by the bathroom door for the duration. If one had a snack, they both had a snack. They took turns picking out what they would do together. If Brittany wanted to play with dolls, Matt had to play with dolls. If Matt wanted to play with trucks, Brittany had to play with trucks.

But, for example, if Matt wanted to play Legos, Brittany usually wouldn't want to but she would begin playing because she understood that the next time would be her turn to choose the activity. By the time an hour or so had passed, the two of them had worked together to create some amazing structure that they were eager to show off. By the time they had reached that point, in most cases neither of them could remember what the fight had been about.

Putting the two of them together like that was so much better than separating them, and thus giving each of them the opportunity to permit their unresolved anger to grow into a smoldering resentment that might have kept them from ever becoming friends.

With only a little coaching from me, those two taught themselves to negotiate and make compromises concerning what they would do together. We never tried to impose a limit on how much time they *had* to spend together, but rather set limits for how much time they were *allowed* to spend together. In that way the discipline became principled and not rigid.

The process of forcing friendship worked with all our children. We would put them with each other when they were having intrapersonal problems, and invariably they would get so wrapped up in what they were doing together that their anger would simply evaporate.

Friendships can be created. We absolutely forced our children to become friends. And they did! I felt it was a personal privilege to be an observer of the wonderful way in which the friendship formed between those two through incremental steps of negotiating, compromise, and finally true camaraderie.

☆ 26

Create Attitude Adjustments

SINCE THEY WERE ONLY HUMAN, at one time or another all the children would have some argument or disagreement. Sometimes the solution lay in simply making an attitude adjustment—bringing about a paradigm shift in the way the child was viewing the circumstances surrounding the particular confrontation.

For example, when Brian was about 12 years old, he would sometimes come to me with complaints about the behavior of six-year-old Malia. Brian often found his little sister to be frustrating. I never bothered wasting my time by telling him to grow up and simply deal with the fact that she was younger than he, because she was always going to be younger. He needed to learn how to deal with the developmental-based conflicts resulting from the difference in their ages. I needed to *teach* him how to "deal with the fact." So on a few occasions I would look at Brian and say, "Are you arguing with a six-year-old?"

He would try to whine his way past the question, saying something like, "Aw, Mom! You don't know what she said!"

But I would only say something like, "I want to be fair…. Are you arguing with a six-year-old?" He would finally get the point and instead of pursuing the problem, would say, "Forget it. It's not worth it." And he said that because he really had come to the point of understanding how ridiculous it was for a big 12-year-old like him to argue with a six-year-old. His attitude had shifted so instead of fuming about the exchange, he merely accepted that Malia's behaviors came out of her immaturity and then moved on.

But that only fixed Brian's side of the problem. Even though he was now reconciled to his sister's behavior, she needed to take some responsibility for her side of the argument. Malia needed an attitude adjustment of her own. So when Brian left I would tell Malia that she needed to stop her irritating behavior. Not because I was going to paddle her or give her a time-out if she didn't, but simply because the behavior was inappropriate given her love for her big brother. "You would never intentionally upset your brother. Right, Malia?"

She would always answer, "Right." She came to understand that she had the power in her tiny hands to simply stop doing the behavior that her brother found so irritating. Like Brian had done just a few moments earlier, Malia came to see that the issue was not worth the fight.

You can use harsh discipline to help children conform to some behaviors or to avoid others simply out of fear. And the fact is, that if they don't grow resentful and rebellious, the patterns will eventually result in habitual changed behavior. But by changing their attitudes through personal choices based on reason and logic, I avoided imposing a standard of behavior from the top down with my kids. All that was required was simply to bring the children to the place where they could see for themselves the futility of their fighting and arguing, and understand that the behavior was inappropriate to the nature of the familial relationships that they were involved in.

☆ 27

Learn to Pick Your Fights

SOMETIMES WE HAVE TO STAND UP for ourselves—create healthy boundaries so we can draw a line and say something like, "This far; and no farther." We have to learn what to fight over and what to simply let go. One of the great outcomes from the internalized attitude-based behavioral choices my children developed was that, by assuming responsibility for their behavior, they learned to pick and choose their battles. Early on my children were able to get past the childish point, which some adults never seem to get past, of believing that every disagreement has to be a battle.

Children and immature adults are much too ready to draw lines in the sand and then to fight against encroachment with an attitude of "It's my way or the highway." But many things—most things, I think—really aren't worth fighting over. We make life more difficult than it needs to be because we aren't secure enough in our own spirit to simply let other people have their way.

The Mauldins have always had a "let it go" theory. I have to prioritize what's important. If someone cuts me off on the road, I just let it go. After all, I've cut people off before myself. If a driver pulls into a parking spot ahead of me in a crowded lot, I let it go. Perhaps the person has some kind of emergency and is in a hurry.

Even when important, if we lock horns with the person and tempers flare, we lose more through the loss of relationship than we could possibly gain through winning the argument.

My friend said that he tries to follow the advice of an old Scottish preacher named Alexander Whyte, who wrote:

Eschew controversy, my brethren, as you would eschew the entrance to hell itself! Let them have it their own way. Let them talk, let them write, let them correct you, let them traduce you. Let them judge and condemn you, let them slay you. Rather let the truth of God itself suffer than that love suffer. You have not enough of the Divine nature in you to be a controversialist.

That's right! I get exactly what he's talking about. However, I've come to admit that the oft-repeated standard "It's wrong to fight" is too limited. Jesus Christ wove some ropes into a whip and drove moneychangers out of the temple when their behaviors had gone over the line. We need to stand up for justice.

People were no doubt shocked because they knew Jesus' testimony up to that point. He was apparently going against His own principle of non-violence, in order to support a higher principle, probably having to do with an unwillingness to step aside and, by inactivity, permit an injustice to continue.

When my kids confront situations of abuse, threats, or injustice I want them to fight. Of course, in almost every instance we don't fight with our fists or knees. "If a person hits you on one cheek, turn the other," Jesus said. But that doesn't at all excuse us from taking determined steps to oppose wrong and to protect the weak. Even though violence is almost never appropriate, my kids might hurt somebody if, for example, they saw a child being attacked.

Parents sometimes elevate the disagreements between children because we're focusing on our own feelings about the issue, thus making the problem bigger than it would be if the focus simply remained on the children. Sometimes they make us scared and often make us angry. Then we commit the important error of responding to the circumstances on the basis of our emotional state, rather than making a reasonable intervention on the basis of our concern to help the children learn from the experience.

☆ 28

Don't Let Other People Take Control of Your Life

CHILDREN NEED TO GET THE MESSAGE when they're still small that the school bully's insults don't matter. They need to learn that the popular kids in school can't define the quality and worth of other children unless the children themselves give them that ability.

It's important for every human being to internalize the processes that create a sense of self-worth. We never will have completely peaceful and productive lives unless we learn to implement Kipling's sage advice in which he noted that his son will have "the world and all that's in it," if, among other things, "…neither foes nor loving friends can hurt you" and "If all men count with you, but none too much."

We need to get across to our children that they should never give over into the hands of other, possibly unworthy, people the decision about whether or not they will have a happy and fulfilled day.

My friend told me the story of three men riding on an elevator. They stopped at a floor and one of them got off but just before leaving he spit on one of the other two men. The third man was astounded when the man who was spit on merely wiped the spittle off with a handkerchief and never showed the slightest sign of discomfort or irritation. "How could you do that?!" the other man shouted at him. "How could you let someone spit on you and not get upset and angry?"

"That unfortunate man obviously has serious issues," the man replied, "but I'm not going to take any of them on myself; I'm not going to let his problems disturb or diminish the quality of my life."

Unfortunately, some parents have a hard time conveying and role modeling to their children that they shouldn't allow the attitudes and behaviors of other people to control their lives. Why? Because some moms and dads are themselves trying to be the popular Kid on the Block. They're in a furious race to Keep Up With the Jones', for example.

Since "values are caught and not taught," as we've said before, children pick up on that behavior and catch that attitude, which encourages them to also get into the habit of making behavioral choices for no other reason than an attempt to win the approval of others.

Our children need to slow down and forget about what other people think. Let's stop trying to live up to other people's standards because there's one standard to live by—the standard that God and the Moral Universe sets for us—that teaches us the high road of love, humility, and integrity.

☆ 29

Have Pity on Bullies (Sometimes)

BULLIES WANT TO APPEAR TO BE POWERFUL, so they take a dominant position over a weaker subject. Pity them for the abject need they have to assert themselves for the fear that they will lose significance if they don't look strong and important by bullying another person. Their attitude is that they don't have control over much in this world, but right now they have control over the weaker person.

Try to help your children understand why the bully behaves as he does, and lead them to consider some kind or generous act. The challenge lies in attempting to do something that will not appear as appeasement, but will seem to be a genuine act of charity. Lead your children in praying for the classroom bully. Help them find creative alternatives. Humor is one of the best antidotes.

Of course, bullying sometimes goes too far and even when you have the mind of Christ there comes a time to strike back. At least don't shame your children when they rise up against a bully.

But know that children who have a central core of inner strength are most able to resist bullies. The real way to stop bullying is to meet bullies not with violence, but rather with strength.

I want my children to follow Teddy Roosevelt's standard: "Don't hit at all if it is honorably possible to avoid hitting, but never hit soft." The fact is, that anyone who practices Roosevelt's attitude almost never has to hit bullies, because bullies only pick on people who don't have that attitude. They can sense when they are in danger of being punched in the nose and will move on. Even in the worst-case scenario, nobody ever has to hit a bully twice.

☆ 30

Use Humor and Fun as Tools for Relationship

HUMOR HAS ALWAYS PLAYED AN IMPORTANT role among the members of the Mauldin family—we laugh all the time. Humor is the world's greatest lubricant for keeping relationships running smoothly. The Danish comedian, Victor Borge, one of the funniest people who ever lived, made a wise observation when he said, "Laughter is the closest distance between two people." To turn the truth around, someone made the absolutely true observation that we cannot really love anybody with whom we never laugh.

A friend once told me that laughter is like changing a baby's diaper because, even though laughing at a problem doesn't solve the problem permanently, it does make things more acceptable for a while.

By remaining alert for the humor in any situation and by laughing at our children's attempts at being funny, we always encouraged humor with our children. But we were also constantly reinforcing the boundaries of humor. We all know that laughter can be as wounding as it is healing. Mocking laughter and humor exercised at the expense of another person's dignity or happiness were always off-limits. However, we never enforced limitations to humor as a heavy-handed rule, but learned to frame it in terms of a question: "What's the most important thing about being funny?"

The kids learned right away that the answer was, "Knowing when to stop." We used the question with a rhetorical force; when we asked the question the children understood that they had reached the limits of appropriate humor.

We even had fun with the question itself. For example, when

Brian was about 21 years old he was cutting up and making me laugh. So finally, I said to him, "OK, Brian, that's enough. What's the most important thing about being funny?"

Brian came right back with the response, "Making Mom laugh!" which, of course broke me up completely.

Laughter was only one part of a principle that I followed to the limit of my time and resources, which was continually and deliberately to enjoy the activities of playing and working together with my children.

☆ 31

Be Friends with Your Children

VERY EARLY WHEN EACH CHILD WAS growing up, we set the pattern of having fun together. I would always get down on their level so I could look them in the eye, and then match my behavior and language to their age level. When they were six, I would be six with them. When they were 12, I would be 12. I continually treated them, in terms of communication, as my peers, which prepared us to remain close to each other when the kids grew up.

We were transparent with our children as well—talking freely about our feelings of disappointment and pride, plus creating patterns of communication that we've preserved to the present. To this day my kids will hug me in public. When my girls call me up it's like a drink of cool water to hear their voice. Whether with one child or in a family gathering, my children are like medicine to my soul. As adults they have become some of my best friends.

Brittany, for example, is now my co-worker, and we labor together to make my new business succeed. It was easy and natural for us to do this because we have, in effect, been practicing for this all of our lives together. There was nothing that we had to learn about relating to each other when we started working together.

However, beneath the deep and growing friendship with my children was my clearly acknowledged role as their mom—the authority figure in the relationship. But there was never any harm in that role because I never used my authority to create situations that would make the child feel powerless. Instead, I used my strength to help make my children strong; used my authority to lift them to a level of appropriate independence.

As a result, Brittany has no problem now with me being her boss. Just like when we were on hands and knees playing Pick Up Stix together, she knew—and still knows—that my authority is a source of protection; that I use it to create a space in which she can thrive.

☆ 32

Honor Thy Children

ANY EXERCISE OF HARSH AUTHORITY is harmful to the parent-child relationship. Parents must exert power in a kindly and compassionate manner. Any display of power on our part was always conditioned by a deep underlying respect that served to maintain our relationship with our children on a level that was fundamentally loving and healthy. Because Alan and I were never inappropriately harsh or severe with our children, none of them ever went through any rebellion against our parental authority.

Some parents—especially some deeply religious people, it seems—place a blight upon their families because they emphasize the principle "Honor thy father and thy mother" for an oppressive purpose. Rather than using their power to create a liberating framework in which their children can develop intrapersonal peace and harmony, they use their parental position as leverage in a power struggle by which they attempt to force their standards, values, and opinions upon their resisting and rebellious children.

And why shouldn't the children rebel when treated like that? Who wouldn't rebel against another person taking away the God-given free will that belongs to each of us? Teenage rebellion becomes a perfectly normal—in some cases even healthy—reaction to parental abuse of position and prerogatives.

All the turmoil and all those turf wars melt away completely, however, if parents will only obey another unwritten commandment: "Honor thy children."

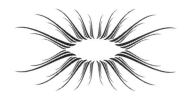

Chapter 5

Child-Centered Parenting

How MANY PARENTS ENCOURAGE their kids to participate in sports only so they can gain the sense of gratification that they, the parents, can receive from the competition? How many parents take it personally when their children fail to compete at a level that the parents demand?

Such attitudes and behaviors are prescriptions for raising troubled youths; these parents are sowing to the wild winds and they are in danger of someday reaping a terrible crop. We can't afford to conduct parenting as an ego trip. We can't make raising our children to be more about us than it is about the kids.

☆ *33*

Provide an Example of Service

ALAN AND I TRIED ALWAYS TO MAINTAIN a servant attitude toward our children, which demanded the the two of us make sacrifices. Whenever they were up with their little feet on the floor, family life was about them. The only break that occurred during those times was when I was able to find 15–20 minutes in the evening to take a bubble bath.

We were not only servants to our children, but we've always brought them along with us in adventures of serving others. We included them in projects for the common good. We let them experience the reality that spending your days in service for God and man makes it easier to sleep well at night.

Even when they were very young the children would assist us while we were conducting church camp or Bible School for children who were much older than our kids at the time. We always brought our kids along for the meals, services, afterglows, skits, prayer times, etcetera. If we were getting ready for a play, I would let them help me make the costumes. They would pick up trash with us. Now that they are grown we still go to things like church camps together, where we create fliers, work on costumes, do hilarious skits, help with the cleanup—in general, just have a merry time serving God and other people.

☆ 34

Make Your Children Feel Good About Themselves

TEACHING OUR CHILDREN TO BE INDIVIDUALS while working together in harmony was not easy. We never tried to promote strict equality with our children such that when one child received some reward or honor we would attempt to give the other children something by way of compensation. Instead, we tried to develop an *esprit de corps* in our family unit so that when something good happened to one of the children, the rest of us would join together to cheer and applaud the child who was being honored.

After all, the children won't usually get applauded outside the home but will more often be ridiculed and scorned. To counteract that, we tried to make home a place where we could rejoice at the least cause for celebration—creating a cheering section to reinforce the self-esteem of anyone who accomplished anything good.

The things you do when your children are younger help them come to believe that they can do anything when they are older.

One of the most effective things I ever did was to freqeuntly spend some face-to-face time with each of my children. I established a very simple routine for making that happen. In the late afternoon when we were all home from school and work, I would cut round circles out of pieces of construction paper—one circle for each child, and would cut each circle out of paper that I knew was that particular child's favorite color.

I would then label each of the colored circles with the name of the child and place the circles at various spots in the house. Upon arriving home each child was to find his or her circle and stay there until meeting with me.

I would then go around to each child and ask about his or her day. We would work together on homework or some other relevant project. I wouldn't do the work for them because it was my responsibility to get them started; it was their assignment to get it done.

Most of all I would ask them how their day had been, and wouldn't accept "Fine" for an answer. If they said, "My day was good," then I would ask them, "How was it good?" and they would talk to me. If one of them would be having a bad day, I would get something they liked—a bag of popcorn or a candy that they enjoyed—and set it by them.

This became one of the best times of day for me. And I suspect that on some days those brief moments with Mom became something that will last a lifetime.

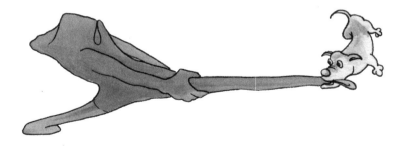

☆ 35

Replace Jealousy with an Attitude of Service

THERE'S NO ROOM IN ANY HEALTHY FAMILY for jealousy, but some families are ripped apart by envy and resentment. And in some cases these negative feelings begin with the parents themselves as each attempts to compete with the other for the children's affection. On the other hand, a friend told me that he would sometimes tell his children, "I know you probably love your mom more than you love me but that's all right because I love her more than me, as well."

One of the little humorous things I did that always brought me a lot of satisfaction was to stand in the midst of my children and ask them, "Who's Mom's favorite?" and then watch all of them raise their hands.

They know it is true that each of them is my favorite because they are individuals and as individuals each could become my favorite in his or her own particular way. And besides, I could truthfully say to each of my children on every day of his or her life, "I love you with all my heart." None of them could imagine that I loved one of their siblings more than them because they all knew that you couldn't love anybody more than "with all my heart."

I remember one day I was lying with the children on a trampoline. We were watching the clouds drift by and trying to imagine what their shapes reminded us of. Malia always saw animals. I was listening to them talk and giggle and sharing about what they saw. None of those kids was correcting each other. If one would say, "That looks like a tractor," another would say, "I can't see how that looks anything like a tractor, but if you can see it, good for you."

I was struck by my admiration for how they had learned to get along with each other—each leaving space in which the other could have opinions that differed. They were able to accept each other unconditionally without any need of trying to conform to each other's opinions, or to try to force such conformity.

I remember that day. Malia didn't say much. She was quiet but perfectly happy because she put her hand in mine and said, "Mommy, don't you wish every day could be a cloud day?"

I said, "Every day is my cloud day. I have you all and you are my clouds. I can see something different in each of you."

Parents often unwittingly mar their relationship with their children by giving the impression that they find their parental responsibilities to be a heavy burden. Children can become alienated when they hear their parents complaining and saying comments like, "I have to take the kid to Little League!" or "I can't do that because I have to deliver my daughter to piano practice."

We need an attitude adjustment of our own. We need to regard the exercise of our parental responsibilities as a privilege. After all, our children are at that point in their lives for such a short time that we should be grateful to Heaven for the fact that we are able to serve them, while we still can play this role.

Taking the child to soccer practice will be a joyful activity if we only realize how short the time is that we have the children with us. "Turn around and they're four; turn around and they're a young man going out the front door," the familiar lyrics remind us, and those lines are not just poetry. Let's regard these acts of service for our children as "get-to's" rather than "have-to's."

☆ 36

Open Your Family Circle to Include Your Children's Friends

WE ALWAYS TRIED TO INCLUDE AS MANY people as possible in the good things we had going on in the Mauldin household and made deliberate efforts to provide a safe and happy place in our midst for the children's friends. I used our home environment as a safe setting where other children could learn and practice social skills.

Our house was never empty and rarely quiet. Our kids learned to be with others. They learned to care for others and developed skills in making and keeping friends. Brian once told me, "Going to school is easy, knowing that my friends were all coming to my house later." And then he added, "I feel like a celebrity when kids ask if they can come over."

When the kids were younger I was the family bus –driver, taking them to soccer games, cross-country events, music lessons, swim lessons, doctor appointments, play dates…. As the children grew older, Alan began to coach some amazing young people and I started driving some of them around, as well. Our circle was wide and open. Food preparation always took a lot of my time because healthy children are often hungry—and teenagers always are.

☆ 37

Treat Family Membership as a Privilege

WE HAVE ALWAYS ENCOURAGED OUR KIDS to treat membership in the Mauldin household as a goal to be constantly worked for. We've raised our children to believe that their last name doesn't entitle them to privileges, but should be something they earn. We're going against popular opinion at that point, because our society rewards lineage, assuming, for example, that a person with a last name belonging to a great person will be great. But that is seldom true because a sense of entitlement is a prescription for dissipation and failure. Each child needs to find his or her own way.

Two carved bears in the driveway of our home represent our attitude about this point. At the top of the driveway, as you leave the house, is a bear holding up a sign: "RETURN WITH HONOR." We always wanted to reinforce family standards as the children left to go out into the world. We wanted them to carry away with them the message, "Remember who you are when you leave our house. Remember that you represent us, and are in the position of bringing either honor or shame down upon your family."

That may seem like a heavy message but it is offset by the other, much larger bear—eight feet tall—that sits at the bottom of the driveway with a sign: "WELCOME HOME." We put it there to welcome the children back to the family no matter the state of mind or condition they might be arriving in. The bear they saw while leaving represented our expectations and aspirations, but the bear they saw when returning indicated that family values and standards provided unconditional acceptance.

We drove home the lesson to our children that they represent us when they are in the world. The things they do and say—the quality of their behavior—reflect upon us. But the fact is that this is a two-way street because we represent them, as well, in the sense that the things we do and say—the quality of our behavior—affects our children.

☆ 38

Work on Your Attitudes;
Practice Continual Improvement

WE PARENTS TOO OFTEN DON'T WANT to accept responsibility for the effect that our attitudes and behaviors have upon our children. One obvious example is that children of heavy smokers have more health problems than do children raised in smoke-free environments.

But the principle operates in many areas of life. How can we imagine that we could be deceitful, for example, and expect our children to develop integrity? If we are grouchy, undisciplined, sexually promiscuous, or unfriendly then let's not expect to raise children who are pleasant, self-controlled, pure, or friendly. It is always easier for a child to respect a parent if the parent has behaved in such as way as to earn the child's respect.

Even though Alan and I have been counseling other people for years and have even put on seminars in other countries, I never come to the place where I believe that I have "arrived." I'm always trying to learn from others—always expanding the horizons of my knowledge and understanding.

Most of my learning has been informal. For example, I always try to learn from other parents. I begin by watching the behavior of their kids. If the children were fussing and fighting with each other, we weren't interested in the parents' insights on child rearing, except perhaps to learn what not to do. And I really have picked up some valuable insights in that way. Most of my learning, however, has come from the parents of children who were peaceable and well mannered. In those cases I've been inclined to find out from their parents anything I could learn.

PANTYHOSE PARENTING

It doesn't matter how long a couple has been married, any marriage is a work in progress. Alan and I lead marriage courses, telling couples how to find happiness in their relationships, but after 29 years of marriage, we ourselves still seek counsel from grounded men and women. I'm always looking for people who are concerned for our healthy growth and are able to promote it.

☆ 39

Avoid Rule-Based Living

I RUN IN THE OTHER DIRECTION, however, in order to avoid the counsel of stern legalists who are trying simply to promote standards of behavior. Alan and I avoid the counsel of people who try to live rule-based lives. We won't let them guilt-trip us; we operate from grace. Good behaviors grow out of attitudes of devotion and commitment; they come from the heart. Conforming to a set of rules can be a deadly thing. We ascribe to C. S. Lewis' position that "Nothing gives one a more spuriously good conscience than keeping rules, even if there has been a total absence of all real charity and faith."

The fact is that it doesn't help any of us to learn lists of things that we "should" be doing. Those "shoulds" quickly become depressing and discouraging. There are probably a lot of things that I should be doing, but none of them matter. What am I actually doing? What do I *want* to be doing? What is the purpose in my life that lights the fire in my bones?

For example, my husband and I don't love each other because we think that we should love each other. Our love comes from a commitment we've made to Heaven and to each other. Make it every day, in fact. Our love for each other grows strong out of our lives of devotion, commitment, and prayer. So we fly to other people who can help us strengthen those foundations.

☆ 40

Learn to Listen

ALAN AND I NOT ONLY LEARN FROM the advice of others, we also learn from each other. One of the best things about my husband is that he has always been teachable. Alan is always ready to listen to advice, consider it carefully, and then, when he determines the advice to be sound, he implements the advice in personal actions.

For example, when Brittany was about six years old she colored a picture to give to her daddy. When she finished she was very proud of her handiwork. She had created her masterpiece. But it was Super Bowl Sunday. When she finished it she took her picture to her daddy, who was watching the game. "Hold on a second," Alan said to Brittany, and brushed her to the side for a while where she stood holding her picture and waiting.

It is OK, under some circumstances, to make a child wait, but I knew that this was one of the times when making Brittany wait was not acceptable. I had seen what was happening from my vantage point in the kitchen, so I called Alan to come into the kitchen for a moment. He came in response to my call, though he did so somewhat grudgingly. I waited until he was out of our daughter's earshot and then said to him, "When Brittany begins liking boys do you want her to confide in you? Will it be important when she begins dating to come talk to you?"

"Of course!" he replied. "You know it will."

Then I told him, "If you don't make a big deal of what is important to her when she is six she won't be coming to you with things that are important to her when she is 16."

Alan marched right back into the family room, turned off the television, and said to our daughter, "Brittany, come here and show me what you have." It took Brittany about three minutes to explain to her father why she had painted the picture and to describe what the various parts of it meant. When she had finished her little speech, she presented the picture to Alan, gave him a kiss on the cheek, and said, "This is for you." And then she took off. She had finished. Alan switched the TV back on and watched the rest of the football game with the picture by his side.

When Brittany was 16 and had discovered the first boy that she had feelings for, just as all her siblings had done or would do, she came to her father and talked to him about her nascent romance. Like all of our children, Brittany had established the habit of talking to her father about the things that are important to her. From the time that they were small, all of our children had established the habit of sharing with Alan the important things in their lives.

Some teenage children find it difficult to talk to their dad about anything important, but my children were just the opposite. They would have found it very difficult not to share the important things in their lives with their father. The habits of a lifetime can't be easily changed, so the trick is to establish wonderful habits of communication right from the beginning of the child's earliest attempts at speech.

Everyone in my generation knows the song "The Cat's in the Cradle."

> *My son turned ten just the other day.*
> *He said, "Thanks for the ball, Dad, come on let's play.*
> *Can you teach me to throw?"*
> *I said "Not today. I got a lot to do." He said, "That's ok."*
> *And he walked away but his smile never dimmed.*
> *And said, "I'm gonna be like him, yeah,*
> *You know I'm gonna be like him."*

PANTYHOSE PARENTING

And then the poignant final verse of the song:

I've long since retired, my son's moved away.
I called him up just the other day.
I said, "I'd like to see you if you don't mind."
He said, "I'd love to, Dad, if I can find the time.
You see my new job's a hassle and kids have the flu,
But it's sure nice talking to you, Dad.
It's been sure nice talking to you."
And as I hung up the phone it occurred to me
He'd grown up just like me
My boy was just like me.

☆ 41

Make Your Children Earn Their Way

WE WORKED HARD TO TEACH OUR CHILDREN responsibility; we tried never to hand things to them. Ours was an attitude given to us from our own parents because Alan started working with his dad when he was a young teen. I recently heard a laughable observation: "If you are working for your father, you don't have a job—you have a position."

It was a great joke, but wasn't at all true for my husband when he started working in his dad's business, nor was it true for our children when they started working in ours. He started at the bottom rung with a bag of trash in his hand, which is also where our kids started. They never got a free pass at the beginning—they got a broom. They had to earn any advancement or promotion they were subsequently given.

We let our kids believe that working hard was a good thing. You start out low but set the goal high. Even if you don't reach it, you made the effort. The principle is to aim for the stars and you will at least land in the treetops. Most people don't make it off the ground because they don't set their goals high enough.

A sense of entitlement is the basis for a life of futility. When Alan put our kids to work in our drywall company, he gave them the same message that his father had given him at the beginning. "You don't get more as the boss's child…. More is expected of you *because* you are the boss's child."

Brian and Matt both started out in the warehouse and both ended up working with the other men on installation crews. They never told anyone they were the boss's kids; they completely bought into what their dad had told them and wanted to prove themselves and to make it on their own without any free ride.

To this day our two sons still work at the company, but now they've moved from the jobsites and are "upstairs" working with the estimators, doing what I call "the Big Boy jobs." They earned the right to those more senior-level positions. They worked hard, learned the business, and paid their dues in full. They've got those positions because they are good at what they do—better than anyone Alan could find to replace them.

☆ 42

Set an Example of Pro-active Peacekeeping

WE SET A STANDARD OF PEACEMAKING for our children and always tried to maintain perfect relationships with our neighbors, even when that was difficult. For example, every Monday night we would conduct Bible studies with 15–20 kids in attendance. The Bible study was from 7–9, but during the last 45 minutes the boys would all play a rousing game of basketball in our driveway.

Our neighbor called the police a couple of times complaining about the noise. We didn't hold any grudges against our neighbor for his Scrooge-like attitudes. The lives of people like that are difficult enough without our adding our own weight of animosity to the burden that they have to bear.

The best thing we could do was to try to shine some light into the man's dark soul. And we tried. I spoke directly to the neighbor, but the only response he made was to say, "It's hard for me to believe that if you have all those kids in that house, something isn't going on that shouldn't be going on." We invited him to attend a session, but he said he didn't have time.

It occurred to me that if we were offending that one person with our noise, we might be affecting others as well, so I wrote a letter to every homeowner within a mile of our house. A mile was excessive but I really wanted to make sure we hit everyone who could possibly be affected. We drove around the neighborhood streets writing down addresses so we wouldn't miss anyone. In the letter we said,

PANTYHOSE PARENTING

We appreciate the support we've been given from those of you who understand the importance of establishing a time for young teens to fellowship, play together and to hang out together in a safe environment. Our Bible Studies are from 7 to 9 every Monday night. If you could just wait on calling the police until after 9:15, we'll make sure the kids are out of here.

We received many letters from neighbors encouraging us and saying that the parents themselves ought to do the same thing. The police were great! They couldn't believe that the neighbor had reported us.

We couldn't simply bring ourselves to ignore the neighbor even though the man's attitude and behavior were abominable, so we decided to relocate to the country where noise wouldn't matter.

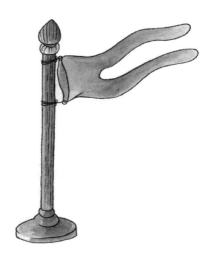

☆ 43

Set an Example of Living Above Circumstances

OUR ATTITUDE TOWARD THE COMPLAINING NEIGHBOR was only one part of our determination to model for our children avoidance of the always-unhelpful practice of guilt-tripping other people, criticizing them, or attempting to assign blame.

The awful thing about those behaviors is that they give us permission to surrender our ability to alter behaviors and attitudes and can do nothing, therefore, to actually improve the situation. By never assigning blame to anyone else we can avoid the possibility of becoming a victim of circumstances ourselves.

A pastor once asked my friend, "How are you doing?"

"Pretty well, under the circumstances," my friend replied.

"What are you doing under the circumstances?" the pastor asked.

Good question! Erica Jong hit the nail on the head when she said, "Take your life in your own hands, and what happens? A terrible thing: no one to blame."

Whatever happens, we have to be responsible for ourselves. We can't assume responsibility for the actions and attitudes of others, but we have to protect our heart. The responsibility to protect our heart rests with each of us as individuals, but the process of doing so begins in the home.

It was our responsibility to show love even toward people who were unlovable, but at the same time we taught our children appropriate standards of protection—teaching them, both by advice and by example, to function physically, emotionally, and mentally at the very height of their abilities and intelligence in spite of what anyone else did or said. Emerson was right when he wrote,

> *Whatever you do, you need courage. Whatever course you decide upon, there is always someone to tell you that you are wrong. There are always difficulties arising that tempt you to believe your critics are right. To map out a course of action and follow it to an end requires courage.*

We tried hard to get across to our kids that the ultimate goal must be to ensure that when they are done with a day or a lifetime, they can look at themselves in the mirror and be confident that both God and they are satisfied with the choices they've made. That's the ultimate consequence.

We will exert the strongest influence upon our children, not by the advice we give, the rules we make, or the discipline we enforce. We are most effective in becoming change agents for our children—or for anyone else, for that matter—by the force of a positive example when we ourselves live according to principles that we espouse.

The life-changing power of positive role models works both directions, because we protect our own hearts as we surround ourselves with people who by their example will reinforce our intention to serve others, and—even more importantly—will encourage us to maintain our connections with the powerful forces of grace that surround us and that are always available to any person with faith.

We are able to set the example of grace-filled living only by remaining focused on the reasons we have for the things we are doing—why we are doing them and the agency by which we are able to carry them out.

☆ 44

Be Creative in Discipline

WHEN BRIAN AND MATT WERE six and eight, you couldn't separate those boys; they were pals. They had interlocking loft beds in their bedroom, one high and the other low, turned 90 degrees to each other.

One night after story and prayer time with the boys, I went to the back of the house and heard them talking and giggling. We never discouraged the boys from that kind of behavior; we thought it was great when the two of them enjoyed their time together. But then I heard something that was not so great, because one of them said, "I bet I can make it farther than you."

My ears perked up and warning lights suddenly went on in my mind. I set down my load of laundry and peeked through their partially open door just in time to see Matthew leap from the higher bed to the bottom one.

"What are you guys doing?" I asked.

Together they answered, "Nothing!"

If I had learned anything about parenting it is the fact that if kids are behaving themselves they will always, in response to that question, tell you what they are doing. On the other hand, if they are misbehaving they will always say, "Nothing."

At that point I did the typical mom thing. "If I were smart enough to know what was going on, I would imagine that you were jumping from the top bunk to the bottom bunk. And you know that's not supposed to be happening. Right?" Both of them looked shocked. "Sorry! We won't do that any more," which was their admission of guilt; that was also the extent of their apology.

I put the laundry in my room, walked back down the hall to the front room where I saw Alan paying bills. I told him what the boys had been doing. "That's funny," he said. "Ten minutes ago I caught them doing that and asked them to stop."

With sinking hearts we realized that if the boys hadn't stopped for Alan, then they hadn't stopped for me either. We were sure that they were still jumping around on their beds.

We went down the hall together, stood outside the partially ajar doorway of the boys' room, and listened for clues about what might be taking place within. We discovered that they had tag-teamed, climbing together to the top bunk, and then jumping down together onto the lower bed, narrowly missing the solid oak footboard. They didn't see us watching them, but froze like statues when Alan cleared his throat. "Did Mom just tell you not to do that anymore?" he asked. And asked again, "Did I also not tell you to stop doing that?"

Then Alan sat down on the bed with them and began talking about the do's and the don'ts of bedroom gymnastics, describing how they might injure themselves. I suddenly had what seemed to me to be a wonderful idea. I excused myself from the room saying, "I'll be right back."

I went to the kitchen, got two raw eggs out of the refrigerator, walked back to the boys' room, and stood there. Alan looked at me and said, "Do you want to say something?"

"I have something I want to show them," I replied.

Alan said, "Then have at it."

I threw both eggs as hard as I could against the side of the dresser. They exploded and made a big mess on the dresser and floor. The boys' chins dropped; their eyes got as big as saucers. They were shocked at my behavior. "The footboard is solid oak," I said. "You can believe that if your heads hit that thing then they will end up just like those eggs. Do you understand?"

They both answered in unison, "Yes."

"OK," I said. "Now you two go, bring some towels, and clean this up." They ran out, got the towels, and began enthusiastically cleaning up the mess left by those two exploding eggs. Once we got that taken care of they went to bed and fell asleep. They never did the jumping-on-the-beds thing again.

Every once in a while, as a parent you do something that you just know from your heart was absolutely the right thing to do. You take some action and a little later you feel like a baseball player who has just hit one out of the park. After the kids were tucked into bed, Alan and I were walking down the hallway back to the living room and high-fiving each other. "We are good!" we said.

And we were, We didn't do any hollering or screaming; we had done no reprimanding or disciplining, we had just used common sense together with some creativity to make a point that our sons never forgot. It just couldn't have happened better!

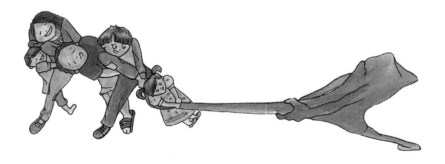

Chapter 6

A Daycare Center Beyond

After Brian was born Alan decided that he had derived all the learning that he was going to get from his 9-to-5 job and told his dad that he wanted to work in his drywall company as a career. That happened during an economic downturn, construction projects were stopping, and money began to get tight once again in the Mauldin household. So I started a daycare center in our home.

The daycare project quickly turned into a real blessing and a source of continual joy. It accomplished the first and primary goal that I had for any job that I would work at because it permitted me to remain home with my child. I took in three other children and from the beginning my daycare was blessed by the quality of the children and parents who used my services.

☆ 45

Structure Learning Activities for Pre-school Children

MY DAYCARE CENTER WASN'T SIMPLY A JOB, but provided an opportunity to guide my own child's development, together with the other three children who joined him in the learning. The kids were aged two to six and I set the daycare up as though it were a school. The day was more than random play; we structured the activities. My family room and kitchen became learning centers. The day would begin with free time, which was followed by sessions devoted to a series of learning experiences.

The curriculum for my program was based on those things that I wanted Brian to learn. My simple learning modules were designed to provide experiences geared to promoting Brian's mental, social, and spiritual development.

I would sometimes promote Brian's sense of logic and reasoning by sending him and the other children on scavenger hunts. They would carefully examine clues that I had prepared to figure out where a particular "treasure" had been hidden. It was a lot of fun for everyone. The children's delight in solving the puzzles and locating the hidden objects had nothing whatsoever to do with the value or desirability of the things they were finding. They simply delighted in each little mystery and rejoiced when they were able to find the solution.

As illustrated by those scavenger hunts, the learning that went on in our home with those four children all shared two qualities in common—they were all fun and the children didn't realize they were learning anything. The first quality was especially important. One of the unintended lessons taught in too many school classrooms is that learning is boring. Some educational programs deprive students of the birthright that belongs to all children, which is the delight to be had from engaging in processes of learning and discovering.

☆ 46

Provide In-life Learning Experiences for Young Children

THE DAYCARE CHILDREN AND I DEVOTED a lot of time and effort to planning and preparing lunch. A lot of learning took place that was centered on the preparation of this meal. The kids particularly enjoyed this because everyone worked together to make lunch happen.

On Monday one of our primary tasks was to work together to come up with the week's menu. We would talk together, taking everybody's input, and reaching a consensus concerning the foods we wanted to eat that week and on which day we would eat each selection. We would end the time by compiling the menu items into a grocery list and after the kids went home I would go to the grocery store with that list and purchase the ingredients.

At that point our learning had only begun because throughout the week we would spend some time each day preparing the items that we had chosen for that particular day's menu. Our lunchtime preparations were stretched by our standard of creating everything from scratch. The fact that this was the cheapest way to feed four kids was the least important part of the experience, though it was a nice one of course. The supremely important quality of the experience came from the fact that the kids were learning about things such as units of measure, counting, processes of food preparation, hygiene, facts about heat and cold, food preservation, handling utensils, etcetera.

I'm certain that our daily and happy chores of cooking for ourselves and cleaning up after ourselves—leaving the kitchen area as neat when we were finished as it was when we started—probably created some habits and attitudes in those children that changed them forever.

Those lunchtime experiences really were happy. We never had to rush mealtimes since we had the whole day, of course; we had time to prepare food right. I'm sure the pudding they were eating tasted especially good because they had mixed the ingredients themselves; the soup tasted particularly fine because they had helped prepare the meat, carrots, and potatoes themselves. The kids thought they were just having fun, but what they were doing was actually Home Economics 001.

Story time always followed lunch. I'm a big fan of getting down with kids at their eye-level, so I would sit on the floor and tell them a story. Then it was naptime. The children all had individual sleeping mats. They would lie down and I would tuck each of them in. After all their work and play, by that time the kids were ready for nap. The hour when they were sleeping was like a gift for me, affording me uninterrupted time when I could do laundry, clean up any area around the house that needed attention, take care of bills…. It was my catch-up time.

Chapter 7

Brian

My first-born child, Brian, was only a couple of years old when I began my daycare center, and that child was born with a servant's heart. He was always a helper; he wanted to assist me and to help the other kids any way he could.

Brian was a child full of energy, but also possessed of a seemingly boundless good nature. He would wake up in a good mood and go to bed in a good mood. He was also precocious. By two years old he was identifying colors and numbers, and putting puzzles together.

It was difficult keeping Brian stimulated because he always wanted more; always ready it seemed, when a task or lesson was finished, to move right on to the next thing.

Boredom was Brian's big challenge in life. The tendency toward boredom is the negative side of Brian's marvelous energy. He could never be content to merely sit on a couch watching reruns of *Gilligan's Island*, and that's a good thing. It's a great thing, in fact! The challenge of maintaining a fresh list of activities that can keep Brian occupied and entertained will always call for higher levels of imagination and creativity.

☆ 47

Get Counseling Whenever You Need it

BY THE TIME HE WAS ONLY THREE YEARS OLD, Brian was putting together 100-piece puzzles. He became so good at them that his interest began to wane. I was trying to figure out what to do with him next. I looked to a preschool teacher friend for some advice.

Earlier in the book, I mentioned seeking counsel from other people as a general principle, but I want to add at this point that we should also be willing to scout out information from others concerning specific questions we might have. We should never be ashamed to actively seek advice from others, and to follow their recommendations when it seems helpful to do so.

Seeking, evaluating, and incorporating wisdom from other people who have already learned things I'm trying to learn, and have done things I am trying to do, has always been one of my greatest resources for personal improvement. People who resist advice and always want to do things their own way without being open to input from others, in my opinion, are limiting whatever they do in a serious fashion. The fact is, that it "takes a village" to meet a lot of challenges in our lives. We're standing on a lot of shoulders whenever we do anything meaningful or important.

At any rate, my preschool teacher friend gave me some advice about Brian and those puzzles that really solved my problem. She said to mix together the pieces from two different 100-piece puzzles and let Brian figure out how to make the two separate puzzles out of the jumble of pieces. So I poured all the pieces from two puzzles into a pile, mixed them thoroughly, and told Brian to see if he could put both puzzles together.

☆ 48

Channel Children's Energies

I BELIEVE BRIAN REALLY DOES HAVE A STREAK of brilliance in him, because before he picked up a single puzzle piece, he carefully looked at the pictures on each box, and then he examined each of the puzzle pieces one at a time as he continued to carefully look at the pictures, and sorted the pieces into two piles, each pile containing only the pieces for one of the pictures. After that he simply put each of the two puzzles together.

I was impressed. I thought his act of coming up with that logical solution to the problem of the chaos of having the puzzle pieces mixed together was a tremendous leap for a three-year-old kid. Some adults might not have figured the solution that fast. I don't know if Brian's mom would have figured it out that quickly.

I'm a great believer in using things in a child's playroom as simulations of the larger challenges that children will one day be required to face. If they can learn patience on even something small—a puzzle, for example—and can step back, take a look at the situation, figure out a solution, make the solution work in putting the puzzle together, the child is developing a set of skills that he or she can later use for facing challenges much greater than assembling a puzzle.

Brian's big challenge was learning patience. The kid was always going 100 miles an hour and running in overdrive. He was no good on the hills. He would grow frustrated whenever he would run into something that he couldn't do right away. He didn't know how to shift into low gear and work on a problem over a longer period of time.

I've developed my own philosophy for life that helps me get through a lot of situations: Life isn't about fixing things—it's about making things work. I try to be proactive regarding issues that arise as challenges to be faced up to and overcome, instead of reactively viewing them as problems that I need to fix. The two approaches may look the same on the surface, but regarding something as a challenge rather than a problem completely alters the dynamic of a situation.

Taking the proactive approach really does cause us to see life from a much more positive viewpoint, because we can't always fix the thing that has gone wrong in our lives, but we can always figure out how to take whatever situation we would otherwise be stuck in and make it work for some positive purpose.

For example, I couldn't fix the problem that Brian was having with impatience. The thing was beyond my control or his because it simply grew out of the way that the child was wired. What I had to do was to figure out some proactive course of action that would divert his impatience into a positive channel.

Once again, the answer came from an outside source, because one day I shared with Brian's pediatrician about how bright my son was, and he made a sage observation: "Brian has something special; the key is not to allow him to get bored."

So I transformed the serious problem into a challenge and demonstrated by yet one more experience that, while a problem can be a weight on your shoulders and waste your energy, a challenge can create the basis for positive outcomes.

☆ 49

Reinvent Solutions

IN THIS CASE THE CHALLENGE LED TO AN amazing outcome, because when we got home that day I told Brian, "Close your eyes and count to 100." Then I took out two puzzle boxes, each with a brand-new puzzle that Brian had never seen before and, while he was still counting, I mixed the pieces from both boxes, just as I had done before. However, this time I stowed the empty boxes, so Brian could not see them from his spot at the kitchen table.

When he had finished counting to 100, Brian opened his eyes, saw the pieces, just as he had expected, but then was surprised when he didn't see the boxes.

"I put them away," I said. "We're going to try something different today. You have to be able to put both puzzles together without being able to look at the pictures."

"I can't do it without seeing the pictures," he whined. "Putting the puzzles together without the pictures will be too hard."

I told him, "Listen, Brian, whenever you think anything is too hard for you, that means it's just right for you." That was a line I often used on my kids. As a result, "hard" was not a word they used very often; the concept was never an issue for any of my children. It didn't matter whether a particular challenge was easy or hard, they learned to just go ahead and get the job done.

Brian spent six days putting together the two puzzles. He would take breaks to play outside with the other kids and would go about his daily routines, but he spent every free moment at the table laboriously assembling the two puzzles.

He grew frustrated and angry. Rather than scold him for his

emotions, I reasoned him out of his anger by telling him, "Getting upset only makes your eyes not see right." Throughout all the periods of my life I've continually validated the principle that people aren't able to see things clearly when they are upset.

Rather than trying to calm him with words, I said, "Instead of getting angry and frustrated, let's take Shiloh for a walk. We'll take all the kids down to the park. That will give you time to think. The fresh air will blow the cobwebs out of your brain."

After we returned to the house, Brian started right back in on the puzzles and before long he said, with real excitement, "You were right, Mommy, now I can see better." Brian thought that it was the fresh outside air that had made the difference! I just smiled. I didn't care why he thought he was thinking more clearly, I just shared his delight that his brain was working better.

When he put into place the final piece of the two puzzles I think my little boy experienced a sense of satisfaction that I'm sure he can recall to this day. The fact is that the hard things are those that give us the greatest satisfaction, because the more difficult a challenge we have to face, the more delighted we are with success.

From the beginning the fact that Brian was such a springboard with a continual go-go-go approach to life created parental challenges. Some parents might have tried to slow him down to a more normal pace—or try to give him Ritalin or other medication.

But I didn't try to discourage Brian's liveliness. My job was to harness his untrammeled energy and enthusiasm and steer it into constructive paths. He's now a jobsite safety manager and when someone challenges him, he's positive and proactive. Perhaps he learned that from the way I treated him. If I had tried to douse that spirit, who knows what he would be like now?

☆ 50

Encourage Skills and Abilities Development

BRIAN BEGAN SINGING WITH HIS LITTLE BROTHER, Matthew, at an early age. The kids always liked doing things together as a family, so when Brittany got old enough to carry a tune they included her as well and the Mauldin family had a trio. The kids sounded great together and were frequently requested to sing in church.

Alan was director at our church camp, called Mt. Gilead, which is on the other side of Santa Rosa, near Sebastopol. People would come from all over and when they heard the kids sing, they started calling us to schedule the trio in their own churches.

At that point we all thought they should have a name for their trio. We sat around the family table one night talking about what name would be the most suitable. We finally wrote the five top names on five pieces of paper, put them in a bowl, drew out one of the papers, and at that moment the kids' trio became "The Growing Christians."

As calls from other churches began to multiply, I created a master book that had everybody's schedule in it. That way, when we got a call from another church, we could check the master book to locate free days.

All this happened when the children were very young. Even though he was the oldest of the three, Brian was still only eight. However, I began to let him act as agent for the incoming calls, instilling in him a sense of responsibility together with skills that would stand him in good stead during the rest of his life.

When a call would come in with a request for The Growing Christians to sing, I would tell the person on the line—usually a pastor—that we were trying to teach the kids how to be responsible and then would hand the phone to Brian.

One day the person on the other end of the line was the pastor from a church in Washington who wanted the kids to come sing at one of the Saturday rallies that the church was sponsoring. "No problem," Brian said. He found a Saturday that the trio had free and wrote down the date. When he got off the phone he told me that he had booked the gig. I asked him what day. He told me and I said, "We have something going on the Friday before."

"No problem," Brian answered. "I booked it for Saturday."

So I got out the map and told him, "Here's where we are…. Here's where Washington is. Do you see the problem?"

Brian put one finger on our Northern California town, the other on Washington, and then held up the two fingers and said, "Look! It's only this far." How long could it take to go five inches?

We gave our children responsibilities and allowed them to make their own mistakes, but we never let them "twist in the wind." Alan called the church and explained the problem to the pastor, who was completely sympathetic with the issue. Alan said, "I'm going to have Brian call you. He needs to learn to take care of his own problems."

Brian had no idea that Alan had made a previous call, and when Brian called the church the pastor played right along. Brian cleaned up his own mess, everything got straightened out, and we could chalk it up as a learning experience.

Our kids were able to learn a lot of things because we forced them to take charge of their lives. On that day Brian learned a lesson about geography, about maps, and about fixing the problems you create. He learned the importance of determining relative positions and distances before committing to anything that would require travel.

PANTYHOSE PARENTING

The story had an even happier ending than that we had been planning a family vacation to Washington six months following that incident and were able to include a side trip to that church so the kids could perform there.

Brian recently thanked me for pushing him to succeed. He compared my actions at that point to those of a mother eagle pushing her chick out of the eyrie, forcing him to flap his wings and learn how to fly. A wonderful image, I thought.

Brian knew that I expected nothing of him but greatness, and would help him work toward all the greatness that he was capable of. I avoided the mistake of some parents in not insisting upon an unattainable standard, which will set their child up for failure, or the mistake some other parents make of accepting mediocrity and conformity that will never drive the child toward excellence.

Brian once said, "My mom helped me to understand my limits without making me feel limited." That was a great comment. It hit the nail right on the head.

Brian now compares his home environment while growing up to Camelot because of the cohesion our family experienced, whether at home or traveling together. I would never permit fighting and bickering. He remembered that neither would I permit the children to be indifferent toward one another. "We had a place where, no matter what happened throughout the day, we loved each other," Brian said. Then he added, "…that place still exists in my parents' home."

In Brian's opinion "There is simply not a more convenient spot for happy-ever-aftering…" than the home in which he grew up and still delights in returning to.

Chapter 8

Matthew

Two years and six days after Brian was born, I gave birth to our second son, Matthew. Brian adored his little brother, and never once regarded a second child in the house as an intrusion.

☆ 51

Deliberately Prepare an Oldest Child for the Arrival of the Second

I BELIEVE THAT PART OF MATTHEW's smooth entrance into our home came from the deliberate preparation we made for his insertion into the family. For one thing, we never let Brian overhear things such as comments about how we hoped Brian would be able to adjust. From the beginning, whenever we talked about the baby we made it clear to Brian that we were extraordinarily excited about the change was going to take place in our family, and that Brian himself was going to share in the exciting thing that was going to happen.

Brian was made to understand that the baby would become a new friend he could help with. We would tell Brian things like, "This is a friend you're going to be able to play ball with. He will help you feed and walk the dog."

We would tell Brian that the baby would be able to learn new stuff from Brian, but before long Brian would be learning new stuff from him, as well. We would add things like, "You can go swimming together with your brother when he grows a little older," and "You can teach him how to put puzzles together."

It was that last kind of comment that really got Brian to eagerly look forward to his brother's birth, because the possibility of being a helper resonated with Brian's servant soul.

When Matthew was born, Brian's world began to revolve around his little brother. He loved him deeply and enjoyed performing little acts of kindness. The two boys shared a bedroom, and when his brother was still tiny, Brian would sometimes lie on his bed "reading" one of his beloved Dr. Seuss books to the uncomprehending infant in the crib on the other side of the room.

Of course, since Brian was still only a three-year-old himself, he sometimes considered as an act of kindness something that an older child would have known better than to have tried. For example, one day when Matthew was about nine months old, I was putting laundry away. We kept a baby monitor in the boys' bedroom when Matthew was an infant and I noticed that coming through the monitor were sounds of Matthew and Brian cooing at each other.

I had thought that Matthew was asleep, so I dropped what I had been doing and peeked into the room. Brian had tossed a dozen Dr. Seuss books into the crib. He then shoved a chair up to the dresser that was beside the crib, climbed onto the chair, from there to the top of the dresser, then into Matthew's crib, where he now sat "reading" Dr. Seuss to his brother.

I should have had a camera—it was a great YouTube moment! Matthew was just lying there, looking up at his brother with an expression that said, "This is awesome!"

At that age, Brian couldn't actually read anything, but Alan and I had read the books to him so often that he had learned the stories by heart. Brian would show a picture to Matthew, then recite the part of the story that went along with that picture. He would then show another picture, and recite to his brother the next part of the story.

Sometimes when he showed Matthew a page, the baby would try to grab the picture but then Brian would say to him with an attitude of firm patience, "No Matthew! We have to read some more."

From the beginning Matthew had an amazing sensitivity about people. When he was still an infant we began to refer to him as "our babysitter monitor." Without being able to speak a word he gave us cues about whether a particular person was a good or bad candidate for child care. Upon meeting a person our second boy would instantly form an opinion.

Early in his life I realized he was able to see things with his heart before we could discern them with our eyes. Besides being sensitive, Matthew was also logical. He could think things through and make out cause-and-effect relationships. He still does.

☆ 52

Respond to Teacher Issues with Grace and Balance

WHEN HE WAS IN THE THIRD GRADE, Matthew came home one day sobbing. A teacher had told him that he wouldn't amount to anything because he couldn't learn a particular math problem. The teacher's negative message was devastating. I held Matthew without saying anything until he quit crying, except for conveying to him that "When you're ready to talk, we'll talk."

At a point like this some parents are ready to march into school and give that teacher a piece of their mind. The urge to do just that was, in fact, my initial reaction to what Matthew had told us. However, Alan and I have made it a practice of not immediately getting on our high horse when things like that happen. When you react too quickly or dramatically to something the teacher says, you end up investing more authority in the teacher's comments than they deserve, even if you take the child's position.

If a teacher in a conference told me that my kids were doing something wrong, we never would say, "My child would never do that." We knew our kids.

When teachers behave in ways that you don't approve of, treat the matter with kid gloves. Don't be too ready to make their issues yours. You're not responsible for what the teacher does, but for what you yourself do.

It's easier to defend a child's faults than to help him or her work through the faults. But taking the time and making the effort to work through the faults can be seen as "pantyhose parenting": it's sometimes difficult and uncomfortable, but the reward is worth it.

Accept the fact that when it comes to matters having to do with our children, we parents are not objective, and some of us are incapable of seeing the situation as it really is.

During all the time that Alan and I have been counseling with children, we've been trying to deal with parents who aren't living in the real world. Some parents adopt the attitude that their kids are perfect when we know that they are actually on a steep slide going downhill toward destruction. It drives us crazy!

☆ 53

Search for a Creative Alternative to Criticism and Confrontation

RATHER THAN SETTING UP A CONFRONTATION that might destroy our relationship with that teacher, we decided to meet the problem itself head-on. The basic issue wasn't a social problem with the teacher but an attitude problem with our son. He really didn't believe that he could do math, so our goal became one of not merely teaching our child to do math problems, but to address the more important challenge of teaching our child that he *was able to do* math problems.

We decided to tackle the immediate, compelling challenge to make sure that our child came to understand that he was indeed smart enough to do math.

When it comes to academics, Alan and I are a good team because we are gifted in different ways. I have strong history and science skills; Alan has always been good in math and English.

The three of us sat down at the kitchen table. I asked Matt, "Why do you think God gave you to Dad and I?"

Matthew immediately answered, "God knew that you would love me the most." That made us smile. I don't know where he got that answer from—it just came out of his little third-grade heart and head.

I told him that it was true. "Do you trust Daddy and me?" I asked.

"Yes."

"I have an idea," I said. "We'll play a game. We won't tell the teacher what we're doing; it will be our secret." Matt agreed.

The game was to prove the teacher wrong without telling the teacher that we were going to do so. Every evening Alan, Matthew, and I played the game together. We helped our son in making up his own homework assignments. We were merely assistants; he was in charge of putting the homework assignment together.

In the beginning Matt always made sure that he could easily do whatever assignment he was laying out for himself. Once he gained confidence at that level, Alan and I began to suggest a twist here, a change there, making the challenge a little more difficult and providing him with the ability every day to derive a sense of accomplishment from meeting his goal for that day.

We followed that routine every school night for the next three weeks—spending 20 minutes each night helping Matt devise his own homework assignment. It really did become a game; the three of us always looked forward to it. As his self-confidence increased, Matt created more and more difficult assignments for himself.

It wasn't surprising that by the end of the three weeks, Matt's test grades and homework scores had improved remarkably. He had become proficient at doing the work simply because our little game had built up within him the confidence that he could do it.

The experience provided another example of us taking the word "hard" out of our kids' vocabularies. The fact is, children can do anything as long as they know they can. Napoleon Hill was exactly right when he said, "If you think you can or you think you can't, you're right."

There were many teachers who had a positive influence on Matthew's development. One in particular, Terri Van Heel, inspired Matthew to become organized and to develop learning skills that, he said, greatly eased his studies in the later grades and in college. She laid a foundation that he says still helps him when approaching challenges.

☆ 54

Let Your Child's Special Abilities Flow

FROM EARLIEST CHILDHOOD Matthew was our troubadour. The kid always had a song in his heart and on his lips. When he was still a child he would perform solos in church. He, Brian, and Brittany formed a trio—and Matt was the artistic lead.

When checking sound systems before a performance, Matt was the person who decided when the volume and balance were in the right ranges. When any musical decision was to be made, they asked, "What do you think, Matt?"

The trio has retired from regular performance, but Matt still performs. He has sung at the Antioch County Fair a few times. During one notable performance at the fair, when he was 20, he sang a love song that he had written himself, proposing marriage to his fiancée, Sarah.

It was a great hit with everyone — especially Sarah!

Matthew has recently thanked me for the many hours I spent with him as a child drilling into him the principle that "hard work beats talent when talent doesn't work hard."

He can still remember disparaging remarks that teachers made to him. Those comments might have affected him and marred his sense of self-worth forever. Many people are living diminished lives because of the influence of people who weren't as negative as that teacher. Matt recalled how I worked with him to prove wrong the teacher's low opinion of his abilities.

Matt claims that he learned from us the additional lesson that God's power can help him through any situation to which God's grace has led him.

Chapter 9

Brittany

OUR FIRST DAUGHTER, BRITTANY, was born exactly 18 months after Matthew. I think my two sons at the time would have preferred to have had another brother rather than a sister, but decided to make the best of the situation by trying to retrofit her so she could be a brother in everything except gender. As a result, before she was two years old Brittany could catch a ball and hold up her end of any conversation about Teenage Mutant Ninja Turtles or Power Rangers.

In spite of all her boyish abilities, her brothers never succeeded in making Brittany into an actual tomboy. She always had a taste for dressing up in fancy outfits; she always had feminine attitudes about appearance and style that related in interesting and often humorous ways with her boyish abilities and talents. Brittany was our little daredevil—she was absolutely fearless. She and her brothers loved to have fun climbing around on the monkey bars in our backyard.

☆ 55

Maintain Your Calm in Tense Situations

I WAS IN THE HOUSE FIXING DINNER one day when through the open windows I heard an alarming sentence: "If she can do it and not get hurt, I know we can do it." I went outside and saw Brittany perched on the top beam of the kids' backyard play structure, which put her about eight feet off the ground. As I watched in horror, she began to tightrope walk the length of the beam from one side to the other.

I stifled my initial reaction, which was to dash out into the yard shrieking at her, "What are you doing? You'll get killed!" I was afraid that if I startled her I would cause the exact outcome that I was so fearful of. So I kept my cool, walked to the play structure, and in a composed tone asked Brittany, "What are you doing up there?"

"Brian and Matt are teaching me about how not to be afraid," she said.

I wanted to throttle those guys, but at that point Brittany and I were alone in the backyard because as soon as the boys heard the kitchen door open they had headed for the tall timber. They knew they had crossed an important boundary; they didn't need me to tell them they had done wrong. Right now I had the situation with Brittany to resolve. I would deal with her two brothers later.

I stood beneath Brittany as she finished transversing the beam. When she reached the edge of the play structure, she stepped off the beam onto an adjoining tent structure, and climbed down the edge of that to the top of the slide. Still cool as a cucumber, my little girl slid down the slide into my waiting arms.

The selfish thing at that point would have been for me to get all slobbery and emotional, and then to give her a me-centered lecture about how frightened she had made me by what she'd done. I could have tried to manipulate her emotions into regretting what she had done so she wouldn't be tempted to do it again. However, I could have accomplished no positive outcome by trying to transfer the fear in my heart into my child's heart.

☆ 56

Reinforce Behaviors with Positive Messages

TOO MANY TIMES PARENTS' EFFORTS to keep children safe are actually intended merely to preserve the parents' own peace of mind. In order to quiet their own sense of alarm, parents over-react and by so doing plant messages of "can't," "shouldn't," and "never be able to," instead of the affirming messages of "should," "can," "will," and "will be able to." We need to try to keep our children safe without sowing seeds of fearfulness, timidity, and insecurity. I wanted my children to operate their lives from a place of emotional security—not out of a sense dread.

So after my little two-year-old returned safely from her potentially dangerous adventure, I enthusiastically told her that she had done an amazing job of tightrope-walking. But then I added that if she wanted to do it again, Mommy needed to be outside with her. She looked at me and said, "Why would I want to do it again? I already did it."

I was so proud of her—not just of her courage, but of her sensibility, as well. I told Brittany to go into the house and get a snack. She skipped away. Now it was time to deal with her brothers. "Boys!" I called. They sheepishly emerged from their hiding place, which had been in the dog run with Shiloh. They had picked an appropriate hiding place—they both knew they were in the doghouse in more ways than one. They approached in a meek, embarrased manner. I sat down on the slide so we could talk eye-to-eye, since a person's eyes can sometimes convey more meaning than speech.

"Who's next?" I asked. They were shocked by the question.

I took them both over to point where Brittany had started her balance-beam walk. "How did she get up there?" I asked. "I know she didn't do it by herself. Who helped her?"

Brian was always the spokesperson in situations like that. He confessed that Matthew had boosted Brittany onto Brian's shoulders. Then, while still holding Brittany, Brian had climbed a little ladder on the play structure so Brittany could grasp the beam and pull herself up to her elevated perch.

"Who's going to go first?" I asked them. They didn't say a word. "Well, if you aren't willing to climb up there yourself, you shouldn't ask anyone else to. Do you understand that?" They both understood completely.

I told them to go into the house and apologize to their sister. Then I made it very clear that they were not to apologize for putting her in danger. It was obvious to me that Brittany should never realize that her brothers had put her in danger. She loved her big brothers and trusted them. I didn't want to spoil that.

I told the boys that they had to apologize to their sister by saying, "We should have gone first, Brittany, and then asked you to give it a try." I made sure they both got their lines straight. They went to her and said their apologies, and then got their snacks.

☆ 57

Don't Force Children into Social Conformity

BRITTANY'S SENSE OF INBRED COURAGE really paid off in junior high school. That's when children begin learning how to pick their friends. Junior high society can be a ruthless environment, even in the Christian school that she was attending at the time. Personal attacks by groups of bullies with the purpose of shaming and humiliating weaker children are regular and uncontrollable.

Brittany was never one of the children under attack, but neither would she side with the gossip and verbal abuse of others. She was unwilling to play the mean little backbiting and gossiping games of the other girls, which was how they maintained an environment where nobody was ever permitted to feel OK about him—or herself. So for a while she had to stand alone.

Brittany was always straightforward in her relationships, both as a result of her rearing and her own personality. If she had a problem with someone, she would confront the person head-on instead of talking behind that person's back. She had an innate understanding of appropriate behavior and a natural aversion to participating in the gossip that was going on around her.

She knew instinctively the lesson most of us learn only through experience—that anyone who would tell us some juicy gossip won't hesitate to gossip about us to other people.

Even though Brittany didn't embrace the social milieu, nor did that society embrace her, those girls needed someone like Brittany. We all need people whom we trust to treat us with integrity, even when we don't deserve it or even acknowledge the role being played by the person they are marginalizing.

☆ 58

Allow Children Space for Reflection

HER EXPERIENCE GAVE BRITTANY OPPORTUNITIES to reflect upon life and to observe what was going on in the world around her. John Miller, a co-anchor with Barbara Walters on the TV show *20/20,* once observed with perfect accuracy that "people who take time to be alone usually have depth, originality, and quiet reserve." That's an apt description of my oldest daughter. She was not a loner, but she was a solitary person when she was young—one who understood what Emily Dickenson was speaking about when she wrote, "The soul selects her own society.… Then shuts the door."

Brittany's social life was made even more complicated when she showed sufficient intellectual and social maturity to skip eighth grade. Even though she had become a ninth-grader at that point, she was invited to participate in the trip to Washington, DC, that the eighth-grade students made every year.

She loved seeing the nation's capital, but the trip reinforced the reality that Brittany really had matured beyond the level of her eighth-grade peers; she and her former schoolmates shared even less common ground than they had the year before.

Alan and I were chaperones on that trip and our second daughter, Malia, who was in the sixth grade at the time, went with us. The separation that had intruded between Brittany and her former classmates permitted her relationship with her younger sister to blossom from sisterly affection to genuinely close friendship.

Brittany and Malia remain best friends. They still rely on each other and maintain the closest of relationships.

☆ 59

Encourage Children's Passions and Gifts

BEGINNING IN THE FIRST GRADE, BRITTANY developed a passion for sign language that continues to this day. Her teacher taught the class elements of sign language because she thought that an introduction to signing would broaden the children's horizons, but Brittany showed such passionate interest in it that I tried to find someone to give her personalized instruction after the classroom introduction was over. I called around but nobody would agree to teach a child Brittany's age who wasn't herself hearing-impaired.

I finally got in touch with a deaf teacher at the Fremont School for the Deaf and asked her if she would be interested in tutoring my daughter. The teacher and I made the connection over the phone using a system that I had never seen before—one that used an operator as an intermediary. The operator would type what I was saying on a keyboard and the words would appear on a monitor in the deaf teacher's home.

The teacher reluctantly agreed to visit Brittany but warned that the interest in signing showed by young children was usually short-lived. She agreed to meet with Brittany in order to evaluate her level of commitment. We scheduled a meeting. Brittany and the teacher spoke together for a while and afterward the teacher told Alan and me, "Brittany has the heart to learn sign language."

Brittany has spent most of her life learning and practicing sign language. She has developed into a fluent signer and has used her abilities in whatever ways open up to her.

When she was 15 years old, we discovered that our daughter had developed into a champion of the hearing-impaired. The incident took place when we went into a Togo's for lunch. While we were eating our sandwiches, a hearing-impaired woman entered the store. The woman had written her meal order on a piece of paper but when she tried to hand the paper to the young waitress, the girl didn't want to deal with her and acted like she couldn't understand what the woman had written or wanted.

The rest of us didn't have the same awareness about the situation that Brittany had. We were oblivious to the drama that was unfolding at the lunch counter, and only became aware when Brittany, who had been watching the whole incident, suddenly leaped up and ran to the counter. She grabbed the piece of paper, crumpled it up, and then proceeded to interpret the woman's wishes to the waitress. Alan went over to the counter and asked, "Brittany, are you Ok?"

"Relax, Dad," she said. "I've got this covered." She waited until the hearing-impaired woman had been served and had paid her bill. Then Brittany made sure that the sandwiches and drink order was right. Before she left the counter the hearing-impaired woman signed to Brittany, "You are an angel."

After the woman left, Brittany turned to the insensitive young waitress and said to her, "The woman was deaf, not dim-witted. Only hearing people who are stupid treat deaf people like they are stupid." She sat down at our table and said to us, "That kind of ignorance makes me so angry!"

Matthew came right back and said, "Jeez, Brittany, if you didn't want lettuce on your sandwich you should have said so."

"Don't start with me!" she told him. We actually thought that Matthew had come up with a pretty good line, but we've always worked to keep laughter within boundaries. The waitress's mistreatment of the deaf woman was no laughing matter, as far as Brittany was concerned.

☆ 60

Practice Absolute Tolerance

WE HAD NEVER CONSCIOUSLY AND specifically trained our daughter to leap to the defense of hearing-impaired people, but all of her life we had mentored her by word and example concerning the importance of treating people as equal and defending those who were unable to defend themselves.

We always tried to operate out of integrity—to be the same at home with the kids as we are in church—plus not acting one way toward one group of people and then acting differently to another. We never attempted to teach our children that they should treat black people different than white, women different than men, short people different than tall, or rich people different than poor—or to use any of the other categories people create as reasons to look down on others.

I think that my children would have met any attempt to convey such a lesson with a blank stare followed by a shrug of their shoulders. We never gave them any reason to imagine that they should treat people differently depending on race or any status indicators because Alan and I never treated people differently on the basis of any of those things.

Don't try to convince your children that they should treat black people the same as whites. Learn to treat the very issue itself with contempt.

☆ 61

Create Opportunities to Promote Diversity

BRITTANY HAD AN ASTONISHING CHANCE to practice sign language when she joined us on a mission trip to Africa. She had been hesitant about going because we were scheduled to get back home just 19 days before her wedding date. However, it turned out that her going to Africa with us was a God-thing because we encountered a young, hearing-impaired African. The young man had learned American Sign Language from a school that he traveled to every day. He had learned to live with frustration because even though he now knew how to sign, nobody around him had learned sign language. His mother and father had never spoken with him.

The young man's plight illustrated a third-world tendency to treat hearing-impaired people with disrespect—regarding them as castoffs relegated to an inferior place in society. So Brittany's appearance at the conference seemed to him like an angel had visited from heaven. She was able to spend the entire day interpreting for the young man.

The way you help your kids avoid even raising the issue of intolerance is to ensure that diversity becomes part of their background. You probably can't take them to Africa's interior villages, but you can take them down to the City Mission sometimes and have them help serve dinner to the homeless. Take them to a black church once in a while. Put together a box of sandwiches and have your kids help pass them out to day laborers waiting for work in the Home Depot parking lot. Use your imagination!

☆ 62

Provide Opportunities for Your Children (not Paths They Must Walk)

WE'RE GLAD TO GIVE OUR KIDS A place in the family business, if that suits their personalities and wishes for their lives, but have no expectations that they should work for us. Brittany worked at the front desk as a receptionist for a few years, but decided that she wanted to be a massage therapist. So she went to school and learned how to provide that much-needed service. We don't need a massage therapist in our drywall company, but we were glad to see her strike out on her own doing something she really wanted to do.

Brittany's selection and pursuit of that profession ended up playing a part in a narrative that reads like a segment from one of Paul Harvey's "The Rest of the Story" radio shows. When she set her eyes on becoming a massage therapist, absolutely nobody could have guessed that I would eventually open a day retreat for women, which was a business that Brittany's massage therapy skills would fit into like a hand fitting into a glove. My husband has been able to enjoy working shoulder-to-shoulder with our sons over the years, and now I can relish the fact that my daughter is working every day by my side.

I know some young women who would find working with their mom on a daily basis to be like some kind of medieval torture. "I love my mom," one middle-age woman once said to my friend. "I just can't stand to be with her more than 20 minutes at a time."

What an awful place to be in!

My daughter recently thanked me for the consistency of my character—for the fact that I'm the same person whether at church, home, work, or the mall. That's a gift we can give our kids—to be predictable and to avoid the hypocrisy of putting on a social face in public that differs from the family face we wear at home. We might fool the people we're with but we can't fool our kids; they will see and understand. When they are young they will find our behavior confusing. When they are older they will find it contemptible.

The fact is, earning the contempt of our children through our lack of character isn't really the worst thing that can happen. The most terrible possibility is that they will imitate us and will, themselves, show a different face to others depending on the situation and the people they are with (also mentioned in Lesson 60). This might be a problem that goes back to our first parents: Children come to imitate the very things about their parents they dislike most. "Values are caught and not taught," as we said, and it seems like sometimes we can't resist catching them—even the ones we don't want.

☆ 63

Lead by Example

BRITTANY COMMENTED TO ME ON how grateful she is for the unconditional love that I've shown to her and her siblings. The fact is, the kind of love she's talking about is a behavior—something you do and not something you merely possess. Of course, my heart is full of my love for my children, but the unconditional part is an act of my will and not an expression of my feelings. I give myself to them as an act of devotion. It's something I have control over; it's something I do even when I don't particularly feel like doing it. This too could be seen as another example of "pantyhose parenting"—the payoff is worth the effort.

Brittany has recently told me that she wants to be like me. She has also expressed gratitude for my participation in her life every step of the way, including attending her athletic events and school plays, and accompanying her on field trips. She says that I'm her buddy. We have fun talking together and hanging out with each other.

Chapter 10

Malia

WE NAMED OUR YOUNGEST DAUGHTER "Malia," which is Hawaiian for "Mary." She was born in 1989 and turned out to be our quiet one, with a demeanor that you would probably call gentle rather than merry. From the beginning Malia always seemed to be remarkably content within herself.

Another trait that Malia has shown since early on has been the ability to be "in the moment" and aware of what was going on around her. On the first day of preschool, for example, she stood in the center of the room with one hand in mine and the other wrapped around her daddy's leg. She didn't care about preschool itself, except she knew that it was in the same building where Brian, Matthew, and Brittany were. The kids all loved each other and she was glad to be with them.

As she stood there with us in the room, she was noticing a kid in the back who was getting into color crayons he wasn't supposed to be playing with. We didn't even know that there was a boy in the back of the room but our little daughter knew what he was doing.

That night she told us all about the rules, including the one that forbid students from getting into those crayons without permission. And furthermore she said that she had learned some of the other inflexible commandments that governed the conduct of the classroom. "When the teacher says, 'Sit down!' then you are supposed to sit down," Malia told us. "When the bell rings you are supposed to line up." The rules were obviously creating a structure for the experience that would have otherwise seemed bewildering to our young daughter.

Malia just had a gift when it came to animals; they always found her presence to be calming. She loved animals, and she loved them indiscriminately. For years her beloved pet was a bearded dragon—a giant lizard that would give some little girls nightmares. Malia would bathe the creature in the tub as though it were a baby, then would dress it up and give it rides on a kickboard back and forth across our swimming pool. Those animals are supposed to dislike water, but the lizard seemed to put up with those wet environments for the sake of the mistress that he apparently loved.

It seems difficult to believe that a lizard could actually show affection, but that bearded dragon obviously loved Malia; he would follow her down the hall like he was a pet dog. Malia would put a cricket on her shoulder and the lizard would climb up her body and roost on her shoulder as though it believed itself to be a trained parrot.

Malia would keep the crickets that she used to feed her pet in a cage in her bedroom, which made the room sound like a jungle. I couldn't have slept a wink in the midst of such a racket, but Malia found the sounds to be soothing.

She also had a bad-natured parrot named Pedro. The parrot absolutely hated everyone except her. Nobody else could feed the bird or touch it. Pedro always objected to Malia leaving the room by squawking loudly, but would remain absolutely calm when she was around. Malia would talk to the bird and it would answer her. She taught it tricks. For example, she would say to Pedro, "Here Kitty Kitty," and the parrot would respond, "Meow."

☆ 64

Share in Your Children's Passions

MALIA HAD A REAL HEART FOR ANIMALS in need and began bringing home stray cats, lost puppies, and wounded birds. Sometimes our house took on aspects of a menagerie or a pet hospital.

The animals required attention and were sometimes a pain in the neck. I never could be enough of a hypocrite to turn them away, however. Because when I was a child I too had a real love for animals. Like Malia I would bring home strays. Finally, when I was 12 my parents delivered an ultimatum, warning me that no more strays would be allowed in the house.

Not long after that I hid a tiny stray kitten in an abandoned tool shed. I began washing my older brothers' cars and taking my pay in cat food. We kept the cat a secret for about two weeks. Then one Sunday I returned from an all-day church baseball game and found the cat walking around in the house. I tried to use my wits and instead of saying, "That's my cat!" I simply asked, "Where did you get that cute little kitten?"

"Don't you 'Cute little kitten me,'" my father growled.

So instead of making Malia leave her strays beside the road somewhere, I would work with her when she was young to help her learn how care for them. One year at church camp, when Malia was 11 years old, right in the middle of a major sports activity, I went into the women's bathroom and could hear Malia taking a shower in one of the stalls there. But then I heard her talking to herself. I called out to her, "Malia, who are you talking to?" She didn't say anything, so I repeated the question. Suddenly I heard a chirp. "Malia," I asked, "do you have a bird in there with you?"

(Pause) "Yes!"

"Get dressed and come out."

She came out wearing a swimsuit and carrying in her hand a small black bird—perhaps a starling or a young grackle. "I think he hurt his wing," Malia said. "I wanted to get him cleaned up before I took him to the camp nurse."

Years later Malia went with us on our mission trip to Africa. During the orientation we were told to stay away from the stray cats and dogs, but while we were there those animals literally found Malia. I think animals can sense when a human being "gets it" about their lives; they respond to Malia's vibrations.

Like Brittany, Malia has never gotten into the foo-foo, girly, gossipy stuff. She will always choose the right thing to do. She was that way when she was little; it's the way she behaves now as an adult.

☆ 65

Encourage Children to Find Their Own Path

BEGINNING WHEN SHE WAS 15 years old Malia contributed to the family business, sometimes doing janitorial work in the warehouse, other times answering phones in the front office. She was glad to do it, but decided she wasn't going to do it the rest of her life because the job forced her to constantly deal with people, and she's always considered animals to be easier to deal with. They made more sense to her.

Malia's purpose in life is in working with animals. She decided to pursue her passion into becoming a vet tech. Alan and I didn't have the slightest inclination to try to oppose her pursuing of her own purpose, or to force her, however subtly, into remaining in the family business. We believed that it was her life for her to live as deeply as she wished. The family resource was available if it was appropriate to her passions and tastes, but we really wanted her to be her own person and to find her way to the life that was best for her.

Before we agreed to pay for her schooling to get her vet tech credentials, however, we asked our family veterinarian if he would allow Malia to work as an unpaid volunteer in his pet hospital—cleaning cages, etcetera. We figured the job would make or break her. After three years she still enjoys serving animals.

It amuses me to reflect upon how much Malia hated working in the dusty, hot warehouse. She objected to the often-dirty environment, but now she's happy as can be cleaning droppings out of the bottom of animal cages—far nastier stuff than anything she ever found on a warehouse floor.

PANTYHOSE PARENTING

One of the great blessings in life is watching one of my children find the purpose for which God created them. Pablo Picasso once said, "Look for a situation in which your work will give you as much happiness as your spare time." That's the position that Malia is in. Her passion has flowered into a profession—today she has a job with a veterinarian doing for pay what she really enjoys doing.

She loves challenges and has ordered her life by the philosophy "If it's too hard then it's just right."

Chapter 11

Danielle

THE WEEK THAT BRITTANY TURNED ONE year old was a big week for us. Putting on an appropriate birthday celebration for our daughter was the least of our challenges because during that week we also moved from our first home in Pittsburg to a larger place in Concord. Even more complicated, that was also the same week that Danielle Weiss—a troubled foster child who would one day become our beloved adopted daughter— moved in with us.

It was a rough week!

Danielle first came to live with us with the understanding that we would be her short-term foster parents. That's what we were licensed for; it was what all of us, including Danielle, expected.

☆ 66

Love the Unloving and Unlovely

DANIELLE BROUGHT A LOT OF EMOTIONAL baggage with her. Through a series of unfortunate circumstances, the 13-year-old had acquired a sense of deep-seated animosity toward everyone, including her family, schoolmates, acquaintances—as well as the series of foster parents she had been assigned to since the day that a social worker had removed her from the abusive atmosphere in which she had been raised.

Danielle was an equal-opportunity hater and she moved in with the confident expectation that she would soon learn to hate us, as well. The Mauldins are a difficult group of people to hate, however. Anyone can love people who are loveable; we can all love people who love us. But people who are walking in grace have the ability to love people who don't like them. Martin Luther King, Jr. was like that; Mahatma Gandhi was like that; Jesus was like that.

Jesus actually went beyond King and Gandhi because He did more than provide a good example. According to my philosophy, He shares with me an actual presence that infuses me with the ability to follow in His steps. The Bible says that we love others because Jesus loved us first. We're also following the loving example of other people who are following that upward path.

The world is full of people like us. A poet name Edwin Markham noted the process of how grace works in this little gem:

> He drew a circle that shut me out
> Heretic, rebel, a thing to flout
> But love and I had the wit to win;
> We drew a circle that took him in.

☆ 67

Impose Discipline and Structure in a Context of Trust

DANIELLE WAS A TROUBLED YOUNG PERSON because she had never before been involved in a healthy relationship and had endured a succession of chaotic social experiences. Consequently, what she needed most was someone who could provide structure for her life; but it had to be a structure that was based on trust. Danielle had to be able to trust us completely before she would be able to follow from her heart the standards and boundaries that we were placing on her.

The components of such trust included our being able to establish a track record of absolute integrity. She had to know that we would always do exactly what we said and that we were always exactly the people we said we were.

She also had to know that we expected nothing from her that we weren't willing to comply with ourselves. For example, when we insisted that Danielle use gentle patterns of speech—not cursing or speaking harshly to other people, or even about them—she could see that we didn't raise our own voices when speaking to her or to others. We ourselves didn't speak harshly about other people.

Competence is the other part of trust. Danielle had to come to believe that we would provide for her. She needed to know that we were able to supply the physical, social, and mental security that had been denied her from earliest childhood.

Fortunately, as it turned out, "love and I" really did have "the wit to win," as Markham put it.

Danielle showed up at our home bringing very few clothes with her—and most of the ones she brought were inappropriate for a young girl. "Let's go shopping," I said. "See what we can find."

"OK," she answered, "but I only shop at Macy's." Danielle's social worker had alerted us to watch for that kind of attitude and behavior. So I laughed and said, "We only shop at K-Mart. Let's go check it out."

But Danielle was adamant. "I won't go shopping there," she said. She wanted to leave the house wearing a shirt that was three sizes too small for her. "This probably wouldn't be the best thing to wear," I said.

"A good friend gave it to me," Danielle answered. "The shirt means a lot to me."

"It has sentimental value?" I asked.

"Yes."

"So it isn't that you want to wear it; you just want to keep it," I said.

"Yes," she answered.

☆ 68

Find Creative Alternatives to Confrontation

DANIELLE'S SOCIAL WORKER, TOGETHER with her biological mother, visited us that afternoon and the three of them spent some time together. While Danielle's attention was otherwise occupied, I put my kids in the car and we drove to K-Mart, where I picked out the best clothes I could find. I sought advice from young salespeople and teenage shoppers asking them questions like, "Would you wear this?" and "What would you wear it with?"

I bought dresses, slacks, jeans, T-shirts—as complete a wardrobe as I could find, with as nice a set of clothes as I could afford. Actually, I stepped out on faith with the "afford" part. We really couldn't afford that big stack of clothes but the people running the foster care program had told us that there would eventually be a clothes allowance.

The fact is, at that point I wasn't concerned very much about cost. I knew that Danielle needed clothes to make her feel better about Danielle.

It seemed clear to me that she wouldn't react kindly to my doing anything to undermine her expressed desires, so when I arrived home I cut off all the clothes' price tags. By so doing I was burning my bridges behind me because if Danielle didn't like them or if they wouldn't fit her, I would never be able to return them to the store. I didn't care; it was important that she not know that they were from K-Mart.

I carried my little subterfuge to the next level by repacking the clothes in boxes from Macy's. Even though as a rule I don't shop at Macy's, my mother-in-law has bought me things from there and I had kept the packing boxes from those gifts.

When the new clothes all were safely stored in their faux boxes, I carried them into Danielle's room and stacked them at the foot of her bed. When Danielle came home she was ecstatic to see her new outfits! She was thrilled about them all, it seemed. She couldn't wait to model them. She put on a slacks-and-blouse outfit that I had selected and came waltzing into the kitchen to model it for us. "How did you know my size?" she asked.

The truth is, I had just guessed, but that question had been really bothering me since, as I said earlier, I wouldn't be able to return the clothes with those tags missing. I took a risk in the "pantyhose parenting" category – this time gambling that the payoff would be worth it. Then she turned to Brian and Matthew, who were still under five years of age, and asked them, "How do I look?"

They both said, "You look like a girl." She took their reply as a compliment, which it might actually have been. And then she said to me, "How do you think I look?" I had been waiting for the question.

"I think you look great!" I replied. "But I have an even more important question for you…. How do you feel in those clothes?"

"I feel great!" she said without batting an eye.

We agreed together that the set of clothes established a good look for her. The fact was, anything that made Danielle feel good about herself was, by my definition, a good look for her.

☆ 69

Promote Your Child's Healthy Self-Image

THE WHOLE CLOTHES-BUYING EPISODE was an important milestone in my relationship with Danielle. She understood that I wasn't going to abuse her or try to force her into actions against her will. Even more importantly, we had made significant progress down the path of restoring a sense of confidence to this troubled human being. It is only when we can develop a sense of self-acceptance that we become able to form healthy relationships with the people around us.

I had one more round to fire in the matter of Danielle's clothing. By the end of three months we had established the beginning of a relationship and I undertook a rather daring project. One day I retrieved the shirt that she had claimed to have sentimental feelings for, sewed the sleeves and the bottom of the shirt together, crammed it full of pillow stuffing, sewed up the neck hole, and thus converted the shirt into a fancy throw pillow.

I felt some anxiety as Danielle came home from school. I was working in the kitchen fixing dinner and praying that my little ruse would work. She went into her room but in a moment she came out with the pillow. "Why did you do this?" she asked.

"You said it had sentimental value," I responded. "You've outgrown the shirt and I wanted you to be able to keep it. But now you can take it with you wherever you go. No matter how much you grow, the shirt will be with you."

It turned out, as I suspected, that the shirt held no actual sentimental value for Danielle; saving the out-worn garment was simply an act of defiance. Her mom had tried to get rid of it several times because it was too small and made Danielle look slutty, but by claiming that the shirt had special significance, she was able to assert her will in the face of the more powerful parental-figure authority.

Of course, when she met me her initial impulse was to continue to establish herself as a person with control over her life, at the point of not throwing away an article of clothing that authority figures wanted her to dispose of.

As had my response to Danielle's unwillingness to wear clothes purchased at K-Mart, my transformation of the contentious article of clothing served to pull the sting out of Danielle's attitude.

☆ 70

Pay the Price for Required Makeovers

FUNDAMENTAL CHANGE IS DIFFICULT for anyone to make. Successfully accomplishing the kind of change that Danielle was required to make was more like tearing out a wall right down to the studs and completely replacing the lath, tape, texture, and paint, than it is like simply painting a wall. She had to change behaviors and attitudes that had been ground into her since earliest childhood. Mark Twain was right when he observed that habit was not be "flung out the window" but "coaxed downstairs a step at a time."

The process of Danielle coming to the point at which she could finally put behind her the earlier patterns of her life was actually like a birth, and it wasn't a particularly easy delivery.

We had a lot of conflicts stemming from the fact that she didn't want to do anything that she didn't want to do. As with the clothing problem, I was continually searching for some middle way through which I would be able to woo her to a set of attitudes that would finally replace the ones she had developed before coming to us.

☆ 71

Monitor and Moderate Peer Pressures

AN IMPORTANT REALITY THAT MADE the challenge of Danielle's transformation easier—or perhaps possible—derived from the fact that Alan was the Youth Director at our church. His influence on Danielle was, of course, enormous. Perhaps an even greater source of power for change came from the fact that for the first time in her life, peer pressures were exerting force in a direction that was entirely different than where she had ever gone before.

In her youth groups at church and in the hallways and classrooms of the Christian school she attended, Danielle found herself being held accountable by young people her age in a way that she had never before experienced. She was with peers who had set for themselves the goal of becoming productive members of society. She was moving among young people who raised the bar of personal conduct and who had high academic and moral standards.

One factor that helped in the makeover was that Danielle is a very intelligent person. She successfully made her way through the painful process of transformation and eventually graduated from Berean Christian High School with honors.

When she was 16 years old, Alan and I provided Danielle with the ultimate illustration of her secure place as a member of our family when we changed her name from "Weiss" to "Mauldin." She was no longer a foster child but had found the security she needed and the stability that, by then, she had earned and deserved.

She became a member of our family in much more than name—to this day you will have a hot fight on your hands if you try to argue with her foster siblings that Danielle isn't actually their sister. She's a sister to each of them in every way but biological, and that one difference means nothing whatsoever as far as they're concerned.

Everything changed when we left our home church and moved to a church in Martinez. After we attended services there for a few months, we became aware of a fine young man named Daniel Prescott. One day Alan pointed Daniel out to Danielle, along with the comment, "He seems like a nice young man."

Seventeen at the time, Danielle reacted by saying, "Dad, that's just gross." I thought it was a great joke that her initial reaction to Daniel was almost identical to my first reaction two decades earlier upon seeing Alan. However, Daniel won Danielle's hand by gentle persistence. As she got a little older, she saw some things she hadn't noticed before about the young man. Before too long Daniel began calling her. One thing led to another, as these things so often will.

Five years later, Daniel changed Danielle's last name for the second time, and she became Mrs. Danielle Prescott.

It is funny how things sometimes work out, because when Daniel was going to college, I was room-mom at King's Valley Christian in Concord—a position I kept during the education of all of my kids. I learned that the school needed an English teacher, and I mentioned that I knew a young man who was about to graduate from college. Through no behind-the-scenes manipulation by Alan and me—nothing but a lot of prayer—Daniel was hired for that job. He then rose to become principal at King's Valley Christian School. Danielle also works there, in the accounting department.

Danielle is now 33 years old and has an amazing daughter of her own, Abigail. The family lives in Oakley, which is only eight miles away. She told me recently that the thing she found most special while growing up was my ability to use my imagination to create happy experiences. She loved how I would turn the playroom into a campground, for example, or create a picnic area under the trampoline, or put on a crazy dance party in the living room. I would make every day a new and amazing adventure, Danielle said.

I guess I did; and it was all fun.

Chapter 12

Finding Ourselves in Africa

Alan and I have always tried to be supportive of our children so they can, in turn, learn to be supportive of others—even of people they don't know.

Brittany and Malia both went with us on that mission trip to Kenya, which I mentioned earlier. We were asked to go there by a missionary so that we could teach people in the churches how to run day camps. Malia saw it as the chance of a lifetime to see exotic animals. We taught some amazing people and witnessed some amazing things.

☆ 72

Lead Children in Finding Opportunities to Serve

THE GIRLS KNEW THE TRIP WASN'T ABOUT US, or about them either. We weren't trying to broaden ourselves or to make ourselves feel good about some kind of role we were playing of bringing help to needy people. We were only doing what we could to help people in Africa to elevate themselves. It is through giving that we receive, however, and the three weeks we spent trying to train people in Africa became a marvelous time in which we learned more from the Africans than they ever learned from us.

The people attending those seminars were like sponges. In their minds the keen anticipation of being able to learn something new justified the miles that some of them had walked to get there. The girls sang for the people and helped the kids with their crafts projects in workshops we gave to illustrate the lessons we were teaching. Malia came to love the people as much as she loved the animals, which was a development that was as extraordinary as it was unanticipated.

Alan taught the adults while the girls and I did lessons with the children and taught them to play games. Not only were we teaching the kids games that they had never played before, but we were teaching them the actual concept of playing games, which they didn't have in their culture.

One game involved the children all sitting cross-legged around the perimeter of a circle, hands behind them, with one child sitting in the center of the circle and carefully trying to keep track of the location of a quarter as the kids passed it from hand-to-hand behind their backs. The kids loved playing that game!

Each game we played had a moral, and the moral of that game was "You don't always have all the facts. If you look for the truth long enough, you'll find it, but you have to pay attention to where the truth is coming from." We drove home the lesson by reinforcing the fact that the only the person who was actually holding the quarter in his/her hand knew for sure where the quarter was—illustrating the point that only the person possessing the truth knows for sure what the truth is.

During our time in the country we were treated as guests. Each day the "mamas" spent all morning cooking around an open fire inside a building that was little more than a concrete shack. The food would never have won awards in any culinary competition, but because of the love the mamas had put into it, we considered it to be some of the best food we ate.

The people in Kenya were not big on law and order. Even though they had very few possessions, many of the people we saw seemed to be carrying firearms. We saw people carrying guns everywhere, even in the hotel where we stayed. I guess if anyone took a shot at them they wanted to be able to return the fire. It felt like we were living in Dodge City in the 1800s, except the local Earp Brothers and Doc Holidays were all black.

During the teaching time on the last day we were gathered in a small building with a corrugated metal roof and siding that the people were proud of. The church was in a ghetto area and during the service we heard some loud popping noise that sounded like gunfire. The people were used to hearing firearms and they took the event in stride. The preacher paused in his dissertation while somebody walked to the back of the building and looked out.

It turned out that someone had stolen a chicken and the neighbors—the equivalent in their society of the "neighborhood watch," I suppose—had been chucking rocks at him until he dropped the purloined hen and fled the scene. I don't know why the thudding of those rocks made us think that people were shooting weapons, but no gunfire had been involved.

The people in that culture were not into vengeance or even into punishment, I guess, because as soon as the thief dropped the stolen chicken, the people quit throwing stones and merely returned to their interrupted routines. Given all the firepower that was present in that little village, the thief was pretty lucky that chicken didn't cost his life.

Brittany was less than three weeks from her wedding. When she heard the sound of rioting in the street, the look on her face was priceless. She had nightmarish visions, like a scene from some violent movie, of being shot to death on the verge of marriage. Malia, however, remained her cool and collected self, and played the role of comforter by holding her sister's hand until the commotion outside calmed down. During their earliest experiences together, the two girls began to comfort one other, and continue doing so.

The Africans attending the service that day remained as calm as Malia throughout the incident. "Go ahead with your sermon, pastor," said the man who had gone to the door after he discovered the cause of the commotion. The pastor started preaching again. Nobody but the Mauldins considered the event to be remarkable; outbreaks of violence were perfectly routine.

Afterward the women and the children gave a final demonstration of their amazing generosity by feeding us a wonderful farewell dinner. When we left for the airport and were on the plane heading for Heathrow Airport in London, we knew that our time in Africa had changed us forever. The borders of our spirits had been enlarged; we had received fresh attitudes about contentment that we never had before—an increased sense of gratitude that we will never lose.

☆ 73

Expose Children to Nature

DURING THOSE WEEKS IN AFRICA we took a couple of days to go on a safari to the Serengeti, where we visited Kenya's Masai Mara. The preserve was off the beaten track and we bounced up and down on the thinly padded seats of a stiff-legged jeep.

We set out on the journey with no idea how long the distance would be or how rough the road. In many places it was little more than a cow path, occasionally marked by holes that would have swallowed the front end of our jeep if the driver hadn't been careful. On the other hand, we had no trouble with traffic; there was no commute on that stretch of road. But it did take us five hours to go a distance that probably wouldn't have taken an hour here, even during rush hour.

Just before we entered the park itself, the keen eyes of our driver spotted something that the rest of us had missed. He pulled over, turned off the engine, and said, "Watch across the plains for just a moment." We didn't know what we were supposed to be looking for but suddenly saw two cheetahs walking together. They both climbed to the top of a massive termite mound about 30 feet in front of us, where they sat down and looked around as though they were lord of all they surveyed.

Our aching muscles and irritation with the dust was instantly extinguished by our awe of being in the presence of those two big cats. It was a breathtaking sight. We sat there for many minutes watching them.

We then drove into the park and stopped at a place called a sopa, which is like a zero-star hotel—a hostel with almost no amenities where tired visitors could crash for the night. We dropped off off luggage and went to dinner, which consisted of pork from one of the local wart hogs, cooked plantains, cabbage, and tapas.

Hunger is the greatest spice of all, so our appetites made the food taste delicious. When we returned to our rooms we saw that each of the beds had been draped with mosquito netting, which somehow made the experience seem particularly surreal—or at least foreign.

The next day we drove into the park and saw rhinos and lions. It was an amazing trip. Alan was hoping for a National Geographic experience—he wanted to see a large carnivore make a big kill. After we had driven around for the day and were on our way back to our room, we stopped under a breadfruit tree and saw a beautiful blue bird that was using his long beak to feast on a nest of beetles inside the tree. "That's your big kill in Africa, Dad!" the kids said.

Alan is a man blessed with a sense of contentment. "I'm glad just to have what I have," he replied.

We discovered on that safari that the African people are more amazing than the animals. I think that's also true in America. My friend says that when he takes his grandchild to the zoo he spends most of the time with his back to the animals because the parade of children, parents, and young people going by on the sidewalk is more fascinating than any wildebeest or rhinoceros could possibly be.

☆ 74

Let Your Kids Learn About the World

PEOPLE IN THE AFRICAN BACKCOUNTRY have nothing, but their positive attitudes made a stronger impression on us than their poverty. Our route took us through Arusha, a village in Tanzania. Whenever we slowed down, children would come swarming from nowhere thrusting their hands through the side of the vehicle. We thought they wanted money but what they were really asking for was pencils and paper.

Those children understood that education provided a path to economic freedom. A dollar would be a lot of money to them, but it would buy enough food to last for just a week, or so. But with a pencil and paper they understood that they could begin to learn something that might deliver them from squalor and poverty.

We weren't prepared and before long had given away all the pencils and paper we had with us. It subsequently broke our hearts to watch the children fade into the dusty distance behind us with their hands empty.

The next day we returned to Nairobi and found a Western-style grocery store. The girls wanted to spend their souvenir money—on pens, paper, and hard candy. When we drove through villages our daughters were no longer empty-handed in the face of eager children; they had educational supplies and candy to share.

We appreciated the opportunity to escape the clutches of civilization for a few weeks, but enjoyed returning to them, I believe, because I think I heard the rustling of angel wings when we found a Starbucks in Heathrow Airport. That was the best six bucks I spent on the trip. Maybe during my entire life.

☆ 75

Lure Children Away from Materialism

OUR EXPERIENCES IN AFRICA MADE US realize that we in America are some of the world's most blessed people, even though we also seem the most discontented. The people in that developing nation and the children in our classes seemed to be able to derive an impressive sense of satisfaction from living. They are more pleased with their meager possessions than we are with our relative wealth. Those poor people were possessed of pride and dignity. They were surprisingly content with life in the absence of material possessions.

Perhaps that came about because people in the African villages that we visited apparently lack a sense competition—they are not trying to acquire more than their neighbors. There is no idea in that society of "keeping up with the Joneses" because "the Joneses" don't have anything either.

On that trip our kids learned the advantages that they have, and came to realize that their relative wealth is not some kind of endowment. They gained a new perspective about the value of their possessions—not simply their cost.

We are still surprised by people who complain about how dissatisfied they are with their four-bedroom house and their heated Jacuzzi. We can't believe how discontented kids are if they don't have the right labels on their sweaters, shirts, or shoes. People in our affluent society don't understand what we have here.

The fact is that we Mauldins were ourselves more contented when we had fewer things. Our kids are still amused when they remember something they did when they were young. They had begged us for months to get them a pool, but we couldn't afford it. So one day when the weather was beastly hot, they found an industrial- strength, 80-gallon garbage bag in the garage. They put the end of a garden hose in the bag, and began to fill it with water. When it was full, all four of the kids sat inside the bag and cooled off. The called themselves The Human Slug. I think they had more genuine fun that day in that bag than they had in the swimming pools that we were subsequently able to buy.

It doesn't matter where you live in the world, kids make the most of what they have. Kids get it; adults make it too complicated.

None of us will actually give up the laborsaving appliances and entertainment systems that fill our lives and our homes, but at least we can come to regard them as just toys. I love my life, my beautiful home, and all the gadgets that I've been able to buy. But they aren't essential to my wellbeing. If my home burned to the ground, God forbid, I would never feel like my life had ended. It's all just stuff, and stuff isn't essential to anything that I truly value.

"Keep a light grip on your baggage," someone once said by way of offering a philosophy for life. It's good advice. I think it's the way we Mauldins live.

Chapter 13
To This Point

I LEARN MORE FROM MY KIDS than from any other group of people on the planet. All five of them were effective teachers using diverse methods and media to bring me to understanding and wisdom. Through episodes of victory and defeat, times when they were popular or felt themselves to be cast-off, through triumph and agony, whether they felt victimized or strong, and in times of drama and boredom they provided wonderful illustrations of the glory, dysfunction, beauty, and intricacies of human nature.

My memories are full of snapshots—vignettes from the lives of my children revealing the fact that I didn't need to study the world "out there" because the drama and issues of human existence reveal themselves in the memory of a two-year-old child weeping uncontrollably over a dead bird, an angry four-year-old lashing out at his brother for eating the last piece of cake, and a six-year-old laughing with unrestrained delight at a flock of geese overhead.

Lessons from my family didn't simply enlighten me about human nature, but I also learned about my women's retreat business from diverse experiences with them. For example, I played with Matt and Brittany helping them put together structures with their Legos, and when I began describing my tentative plans, they listened to me; they actually heard me when I told them, "It would be so cool to have a place of my own."

In their creative innocence, the two children were so visual that they began instantly to picture the dream facility I was describing. I told them my idea of having design themes around birdhouses and butterflies. Brian found lamps in the catalog featuring those designs; we just had to have them.

On warm, rainy days we would put on boots and splash around in the water, but when the weather turned cold and we had to stay inside, I thought of how nice it would have been to enjoy the sound of the rain even when sitting indoors. That formed the genesis of our enclosed garden and fountain.

In the car when things got noisy I would pop in an instrumental CD and play it in the background as a way of creating a soothing effect on everyone. Without me saying a word the kids would calm down; the noise and racket in the car would fade. The kids had no idea what was happening, but the experience illustrated the power of music "to sooth the savage beast."

The things I was trying to teach my kids when they were young have come full circle. Now I often find myself engaged in situations of role reversal, because I'm learning more from them than they're learning from me.

Some lessons have been uncomfortable; at times I'm irritated by their reactions to my particular issues or problems. But the worst part is that when I'm being honest, I have to admit that their most annoying reactions turn out to be the very reactions that I would have had myself if the situation were reversed. In fact, those were indeed the very reactions I had when the situations *were* reversed.

It feels good to be surrounded by these children of ours—Brian with his lovely Lauren; Matthew sharing his life with sweet Sarah; Brittany with her great protector, Dustin; Malia and her quiet strength; Danielle with her caring Dan and my buddy, Abby. How blessed I am to have my kids actually starting to take care of me.

I want to acknowledge the importance of the people who have married and are marrying our children. I started praying for these people when each of the kids was still in my womb. While they were growing up I would take time to pray for the child who was also growing somewhere whom they would one day marry.

When the kids were younger Brian and Matthew went to school with the two girls they would marry. They began with high school infatuations that blossomed into romance. Sarah and Brian carpooled to Hayward State. Matt and Lauren also carpooled to DVC and then to Hayward State, which was a crossover because Brian was dating Lauren and Matt was dating Sarah. Each boy completely entrusted his girlfriend to his brother. It was wonderful because those two guys were more trustworthy than any stranger could or would have been. Through a series of dramas Sarah and Lauren became best friends, and remain so today.

We were teaching at a young-adult retreat when Dustin came to Alan and me, telling us how a girl had broken his heart. We told him, "Life happens that way sometimes. We'll pray with you about that." Brittany was also at the retreat but Dustin didn't give her the time of day. Brittany, however, had noticed him and asked us to pray that she could get to know him better. She said she thought she liked him. We knew, of course, what Dustin and told us not long before, but kept mum. It wasn't Brittany's business.

Five months later at church camp, Dustin finally noticed Brittany. Alan and I soon saw the extent that both of them were "noticing" each other—spending time together at meals, chapel, etcetera. On Thursday night Dustin was running down a path to get something from his cabin. He stopped me. "Sister Geri, why didn't you tell me your daughter was so amazing!!"

"That was something you need to see for yourself!" I said.

When we were leaving on Saturday to drive home, Dustin approached Alan and asked if he could call Brittany. Alan, being who he is, asked him, "What do you want to call her?" But then he smiled and said, "Of course you can." He knew that Dustin lived four hours from us, which provided a measure of security.

Brian and Lauren got married in a small, intimate service in

Maui with the waves crashing in the background. By contrast, Matt and Sarah had a large church wedding in March with a winter theme (including artificial snow and all the bridesmaids accessorized with little muffs). Brittany and Dustin were married at Oakland's historic Dunsmuir Mansion. Dustin was a prince and Brittany was his princess making a grand entrance riding in a horse-drawn carriage and adorned with a dress that seemed like something out of the ballroom scene in *Cinderella*. Danielle and Dan had a big church wedding in Concord with a lavish reception sponsored by a group of church members and featuring the theme "A Walk in the Park."

Alan and I both love all our kids' spouses. and we all get along. The couples now married include Malia; they often get together Sunday night after church. Malia in her mature and sweet nature makes it easy for her older siblings to share their lives with her. They encourage her as she completes a two-year course to become a vet tech in a nearby college; her hope is then to attend U.C. Davis in Sacramento. She works, goes to school, goes to church, and stays on the task. Ask her about her relationship with God. She has no problem talking about what He means to her.

Grandchildren are now starting to show up and my children will begin passing along the wisdom, positive attitudes, and patterns of behavior that they received from me and their father. I'm part of an unbounded and expanding circle of life as principles and lessons that I've received are being passed on to others—to the children who follow after me, to the parents and young people with whom I counsel, and through this book to you, dear reader.

Appendix A
Come to My Garden

I PROVIDE A SERVICE FOR WOMEN that is as perfectly unique as it is absolutely wonderful. My **Cabanas in the Garden** is a place where serenity meets sanity—a day retreat for women in which I am providing a unique solution to the problem that most of us women have—finding time for ourselves during which we can recharge our batteries.

Some women neglect their need for renewal because of the fear of appearing self-indulgent. However, the ability to periodically escape from the cares and responsibilities of life serves to enhance a woman's ability to care for others, which, after all, is our birthright and the natural outworking of our nurturing instincts.

Our local Better Business Bureau had trouble fitting Cabanas into a category so they listed it in the Health and Wellbeing industry. That's an appropriate designation.

Introduction

MY PERSONAL CONVICTIONS CONTRIBUTED to my vision for the Cabanas. I'm seeking to follow the Bible's heavenly instruction: "Be still and know that I am God." The fact is that there's an empty place inside each of us that can only be filled during times when we are alone with our reflections and meditations; times when we can be still in the presence of our God, however we understand what that actually means.

After all, the Bible says that God Almighty, himself, took a break after working for a whole week. Only by taking care of ourselves are we able to care for the wellbeing of those around us without becoming bitter and cranky.

Our need for times of stillness isn't associated with any sectarian religious point-of-view. Whether Christian, Jewish, Mormon, Buddhist, or Atheist, I don't know any woman, whatever her worldview, who doesn't agree that productivity is improved when given a time and place where we can just be quiet—some time to withdraw from the cares and concerns of life.

Life steals this important time from us. We don't mean for it to happen—nor are we even particularly aware when personal time has gone; we simply come to the point where we realize that we're frazzled. The unending round of responsibilities and unceasing daily tasks has worn us down and stolen the joy from our lives.

Women use various methods to try to solve the problem of finding necessary personal time. Sometimes we go shopping, take a bath, work in the yard, or read a book. Any of these can help, but often imperfectly. Issues with traffic, weather, intrusive family members, pests, and noisy neighbors can turn our attempts to find serenity into emotionally draining experiences.

The fact is, Oprah was just wrong when she said that a woman can make a spa area in her home. Oprah couldn't understand about kids dumping things into the toilet, crawling into forbidden spaces in the kitchen, or banging their knees on the sidewalk.

Cabanas in the Garden provides a perfect solution to our need to periodically remove ourselves from the cares of life. There's not another place like it in the world.

Plus, the road that brought me to the point where I could first envision and then actually build and this lovely facility is as unique as the venue itself.

I hope and pray that as you read my story you will have your conviction restored that a life of constant renewal and peace is not only what you deserve, but is something you can possess as you find your own getaway where you can replenish the streams of energy feeding your own life and soul.

The Cabanas Solution

THE ORIGINAL IDEA FOR CABANAS IN THE GARDEN came to me when my husband and I were vacationing at a Hawaiian resort. We were staying in a cabana next to the beach.

I had a sudden epiphany of a wonderful place where a woman wouldn't have to worry about sunburn, or whether a wave would take one of her kids away, or how to clean up the mess after the youngest one dumped a whole can of Coke down the front of his shirt. I spent the next decade figuring out how to provide this for women.

Cabanas in the Garden offers absolutely unique features. The "Garden" referred to in its title fills the main interior space.

It is a great moment when people turn the corner from the lobby and catch their initial glimpse of the Garden. In many cases they actually gasp. Some say they get goose pimples. Even though it is fully enclosed, passing from the lobby into the Garden is like stepping into a gracious outdoor courtyard.

A large fountain in the Garden heightens the sense of being outdoors. The fountain is eight feet high and bathes the entire environment with the soothing sounds of flowing water.

Everything around the fountain is what you would find in a garden area at a fine resort. A stately garden clock enhances the sensation of being outdoors and an ornate archway frames a beautiful mural on the back wall. There are three separate spacious seating areas on the Garden deck, each equipped with a set of absolutely comfortable lounges and chairs.

Women love to recline on those chairs. They set back in their plush robes and warm slippers, sometimes reading or simply staring into the mural's scene depicting a rural tropical area including a hammock that begins to call to the women who look at it long enough.

The Garden area provides spaces for women to visit in small groups or to curl up by themselves with a book or magazine and, soothed by the strains of the ethereal music and by water splashing in the fountain, to simply shut the world out for a while.

A real non-operating phone booth enhances the outdoor feel of the interior space. The amazingly cute booth, called a Tele-box, was an English import. Cell phone use is prohibited but the staff understands the need to use these sometimes. They tell guests to put their cell phones on vibrate and to talk on their cell phones only in the booth.

A dozen rooms—the cabanas themselves—are spaced around the central courtyard. Cabanas provides spa-type treatments but unlike spas, women can spend time as they wish in a pleasant personal space.

The Cabanas experience is one of unbroken serenity right

from the start and typically offers treatments only after a woman has brought herself into a serene state of mind. The distinction is important because a woman in a state of serenity has prepared herself to enjoy the full effects of any spa treatment.

Four of the cabanas are treatment rooms where a skilled esthetician does facials. Plus, Cabanas in the Garden offers every type of massage, including lomi lomi, which is an amazing Hawaiian technique centered around a continual series of massage motions—like waves on a beach. So relaxing!

They offer hot stone massages and aromatherapy treatments, plus a pre-natal massage—performed on a special table. Paraffin treatments involve wrapping warm bags of wax around the extremities, which are then enclosed in booties and mittens to soften the hands and feet, followed by an exfoliating scrub.

Most of the treatments can be done in the Garden, if clients prefer. A chair massage is available for a quick pick-me-up.

The other eight cabanas are central to my vision. Two of them are suites with flat-screen televisions and Jacuzzi tubs. These are available for bubble baths in which women can sink down in the tub without a child knocking on the door and shouting, "What are you doing in there?" Or, as one woman told us, sticking their little fingers beneath the bathroom door and wiggling them at their mom, who was desperately trying to soak in the tub.

The cabanas provides the "me" time that women need. Women can retreat into these for a time alone. We knock on the door ten minutes before the time is up and women often say, "Already? That went so fast!"

Some of our clients come in for a Book Club experience, meaning they simply come to the Cabanas to read. Some bring their own book from home or else they borrow one of our books. They will curl up with a cup of hot tea or a snack we provide from

Willy's Bagels and read to their heart's content. When women leave they can mark the place in the book for the staff to put into the book vault to have ready for the next time they come in.

Some women come in on a regular basis just to renew themselves and prepare themselves to face life once again. They are making intelligent choices in not permitting themselves to be overwhelmed by daily routines; they are regularly replenishing the wellsprings of life so that they can return to their lives of service with cheerful hearts.

Cabanas in the Garden hosts wedding showers, baby showers, girls' nights out, and office parties. Thirteen women from a local dental group recently came in, put on robes and slippers, and then sat around talking uninterrupted.

Cabanas in the Garden is like a dream come true for many of our clients. I hear that refrain over and over.

Genesis of the Garden

I LEARNED FROM WATCHING MY MOM raise six children how important and even precious periodic times away from the pressures of life can be.

I raised five children of my own: two sons and three daughters. Since 1988 my husband and I have been operating a company in Concord called Pace Drywall. This has become a family affair because our two sons, two daughters-in-law, and a son-in-law are on the company payroll.

As my children grew older, I began the journey that brought me to Cabanas in the Garden by spending 15 years collecting information from women and talking with spa owners about what women needed, wanted, and enjoyed the most.

I created the Cabanas with no formal qualifications as a

designer. What I understand is women. My association with Alan's activities and with our company resulted in my being continually surrounded by married women, single moms, maiden aunts, and grandmothers—many of them stressed out by the pace of the world and the demands placed on their lives.

I've been to London, Italy, and France and discovered that wherever you go, women are seeking a quiet, private place where they can simply breathe. My husband and I have conducted seminars on relationships in Kenya, where I spent a lot of time with the women, called mamas. These women were also often overwhelmed by their responsibilities. Like their sisters in America and Europe, they cherished their children and didn't want to avoid family responsibilities, but needed occasional breaks from the incessant demands family and society placed on them.

Cabanas in the Garden resulted from a lot of prayer. I developed a goal to provide a place where woman could be comfortable. I regard the Cabanas as a ministry.

We recently blocked off a time for the women residents from a local battered women's shelter. We served the ladies a light lunch and permitted them to simply sit and talk together in the Garden. When they left I noticed that each of the women had an expression on her face different then the one she came in with. The time apart had softened their features because of the peace that the experience had brought to their hearts.

Cabanas in the Garden is surely a God-thing, but nothing about it is religious. I'm merely restoring to women their right to experience the peace that the world has taken from them—providing women with a place to catch their spiritual breath.

Geri and Brian Mauldin (page 111)

Geri and Matthew Mauldin (page 121)

Brittany (Mauldin) Wright (page 131)

Malia Mauldin (page 145) and Geri

Geri and Daneille (Mauldin) Prescott (page 153)

Geri and granddaughter Abigail Prescott (page 163)

Geri and Alan Mauldin (page 13)

Dustin Wright, Lauren (Smith) Mauldin, Geri Mauldin,
Sarah (Snedeker) Mauldin, Dan Prescott

Author Elizabeth (Geri) Mauldin

— BOOK ORDER FORM —

Pantyhose Parenting

ISBN 978-1-935530-00-8

Please send me:

Number of books _____ @ $19.25 each = _____

Sales Tax (add 9.25% for books shipped to CA) = _____

Shipping/Handling (add $5 for first book) = _____

Add $1 for each add'l book to same address = _____

Total Enclosed = _____

Check or money order payable to ELIZABETH MAULDIN.

Send to (please print):

Name _____

Address _____

City _____

State, Zip Code _____

Send your payment with a photocopy of this order form to:

4353 Briones Valley Rd., Brentwood, CA 94513.

Books will be shipped within two weeks on receipt of order.

Thank you.